THE MYSTERY OF
PROVIDENCE

The Mystery of Providence

JOHN FLAVEL

I will cry unto God most High ; unto God that performeth all things for me.
(Psalm 57. 2)

THE BANNER OF TRUTH TRUST
78b Chiltern Street, London, W1

First published 1678
First Banner of Truth Trust edition 1963

Set in 10 pt Pilgrim, 1¼ pts leaded
Printed and bound in Great Britain by
Hazell Watson & Viney Ltd
Aylesbury and Slough

CONTENTS

PUBLISHERS' INTRODUCTION

O N 13th February, 1688,* amidst the splendour of the Banqueting House at Whitehall an epoch-making event took place. Prince William and Princess Mary of Orange accepted the Crown from the estates of England. They were proclaimed as King and Queen; 'Thus,' in the words of Lord Macaulay, 'was consummated the English Revolution.' Throughout the land the following day was observed as a public thanksgiving for the deliverance of the nation from Papacy. Preaching at this celebration, one of the few surviving Puritan leaders, John Flavel, had occasion to observe a remarkable coincidence. In 1588 England had experienced a signal deliverance from Roman Catholicism. The mighty Armada of Spain, sent to dethrone the Protestant Elizabeth and restore her people to the 'old faith', had been blasted by the winds and waves. A hundred years had passed, Flavel reminded his hearers. 'Yet behold another *Eighty-eight* crowned and enriched with mercies, no less admirable and glorious than the former.' Another attempt to subjugate England to the yoke of Rome had been thwarted by the Providence of God.

The century spanned by the Spanish Armada and the 'Glorious Revolution' was as decisive in the religious as in the political history of England. The religions of Rome and of the Reformation were locked in a struggle for national supremacy. 1662 saw the expulsion from the national Church of the Puritans, those who above all stood for the Reformation principle of the supremacy of Scripture in the Church. In 1688 the claim of Roman Catholicism

* This date is sometimes given as 1689. Until 1751, 25th March was reckoned as the first day of the legal year; thereafter 1st January became the official date. Thus what Flavel and his contemporaries called 13th February, 1688, would, according to our modern style of reckoning, be classed as 1689.

to be the religion of England was, for generations to come, re-pudiated. This did not mean, however, the triumph of Puritanism. Indeed, it would be true to say that by 1688 the Puritan move-ment was virtually at an end. Its aims were to a large extent still unrealized.

The history of Puritanism is quite remarkable. As a movement for thorough reform of the Church on the basis of the Word of God, it was indeed as old as the Reformation. But if the Reforma-tion revived preaching, the Puritans came to stand for preaching of a particular kind. It has been the verdict of competent judges ever since that, for applying the Word of God to the conscience with power, thoroughness and unction, the Puritans stand alone. Yet it is difficult to define in detail how they differ from preachers of other ages. It is as difficult to explain how the movement arose, in a short time producing a host of outstanding preachers, and then, a hundred years or so later, how this supply dried up. If we take the view that the Puritan movement was nothing less than an outpouring of the Holy Spirit upon the Church in England, then it is a signal instance of the principle of divine working enunciated by our Lord : 'The wind bloweth where it listeth, and thou hearest the sound thereof, but canst not tell whence it cometh, and whither it goeth. . . .'

This view of the Puritan movement as pre-eminently God-given is borne out by the absence of anything in the nature of a gradual decline in the calibre of the Puritans. One of the most noteworthy of the later Puritans, John Flavel of Dartmouth, will bear com-parison as a practical writer with any of his predecessors, though by far the greater part of his ministry fell after the Great Ejection of 1662. His father, Richard Flavel, was minister at Bromsgrove in Worcestershire, and from all accounts a faithful servant of God. His ministry, like many others, was terminated by law in 1662 and he died prematurely of the plague in 1665, after being imprisoned in Newgate on a charge of sedition. John was the eldest son in a Puritan household and like many similarly placed, he was sent to university at what would now be considered an early age, entering University College, Oxford. The visitation of Oxford ordered by Parliament in 1647, after the first civil war, and the consequent reorganization of the university took place almost certainly while

Flavel was there. Speaking of his time at Oxford, Flavel regretted that he had neglected the good of his own soul so much. None the less, in 1650 he was recommended as assistant to the minister of Diptford, Devon, and so commenced his life's work.

Mr Walplate, the rector of Diptford, had sought help because of failing health. Consequently his young assistant was not starved of ministerial duties. Flavel was formally ordained to the ministry in October 1650. Hearing of an ordination service at Salisbury, he offered himself there for examination by the Presbytery and was duly recognized. Though he succeeded Walplate as rector of Diptford on the latter's death and was comparatively well-paid, Flavel accepted a call to another sphere of service in 1656. The seaport of Dartmouth in Devon could look back upon a long history. From an early period it was noted for its capacious harbour, and in 1190 had been the rendezvous of the Crusading Fleet. Coming down to the seventeenth century, it was an important post in the Civil War, captured for the king by Prince Maurice after a siege of four weeks in 1643 and retained by the Royalists until 1646, when it was taken by General Fairfax. In 1656, Anthony Hartford, minister of Dartmouth, died. Two churches were associated in the incumbency, St Saviour's and Townstall. To St Saviour's the inhabitants chose Allan Geare, son-in-law of the famous John Canne, pastor of the English church at Amsterdam. As Hartford's successor at Townstall church a young man was designated who had recently presided with distinction at a provincial synod of the Devonshire churches. That young man was John Flavel, and so commenced an association with Dartmouth which continued until his death.

Flavel's ministry at Dartmouth might well have been attended by great outward prosperity and success had it fallen in another era. In fact, like many others, including his own father, he was ejected by the Act of Uniformity in 1662. This enactment was successful in silencing some of the nonconforming ministers. Many, however, considered that their divine commission took precedence over any man-made laws. Thus Flavel continued to exercise his ministry in Dartmouth as he was able. Not satisfied with the ejection, the government of Charles II sought to destroy Dissent altogether. In 1665 the Oxford Act forbade nonconforming ministers to come within five miles of a town unless they took an oath, including a promise not to endeavour any alteration in church or state. Some of the nonconformists in Devon, notably John Howe, took the oath. Flavel, however, refused to do so, though this meant leaving his home and flock. Moving to Slapton, a village which was the prescribed distance from Dartmouth, he was resorted to by many of his old parishioners, to whom he preached on Sundays. A brief respite for the Puritans followed upon the Declaration of Indulgence issued by Charles II in 1672. The king, unknown to the nation and to Parliament, had entered into an engagement with Louis XIV of France to establish Roman Catholicism in England, and as a preliminary step, granted liberty of worship to dissenters, Protestant and Roman Catholic. Flavel took advantage of this liberty and was licensed as a Congregationalist. Even when, shortly afterwards, the Indulgence was withdrawn as a result of parliamentary pressure, he continued to preach in Dartmouth. He preached in private houses and woods and even held meetings at low water on a rock called Saltstone in Kingsbridge estuary.

As a leading and active Nonconformist, Flavel was often in danger and in 1682 was compelled to leave Dartmouth for London. In the city he met with other dissenting ministers, notably William Jenkyn. In September 1684, Jenkyn, Flavel and other friends were gathered for prayer when soldiers broke in upon them. Jenkyn was arrested and though Flavel managed to escape he was close enough to hear the soldiers' insolence to their captive. He returned to Devon soon after this experience, refusing an invitation to succeed Jenkyn, who died in prison in January 1685. Flavel lived to enjoy the liberty given to dissenters by the last Stuart king, James II, and rejoiced in the bloodless revolution of 1688-9, which made the English crown Protestant and gave lasting toleration to nonconformists. At this time measures were afoot to settle the differences between the Presbyterians and Congregationalists. This work was dear to Flavel's heart and he played a leading role in promoting the 'Happy Union' in Devon. It was while engaged in this work that he died suddenly at Exeter in 1691. He was buried at Dartmouth, 'being accompanied to his grave by many dissenters', says an unsympathetic witness. It is recorded that in 1709 his epitaph was removed. The vicar objected to it as being worthy of a bishop.

Even a brief glance at Flavel's history gives some indication of his outstanding character. Of his influence, Wood, the Royalist historian, observes that he had more disciples than either John Owen or Richard Baxter. The same writer accused him of plagiarism, sedition and faction. It seems, however, that to Wood his great crime was that he did not conform in 1662. One who was intimately acquainted with him, John Galpine of Totnes, draws attention in his memoir of Flavel to three characteristics, his diligence, his longing for the conversion of souls and his peaceable and healing spirit. In addition to the incidents recorded in his own writings, there are some remarkable examples of the effects of Flavel's ministry. Luke Short was a farmer in New England who attained his hundredth year in exceptional vigour though without having sought peace with God. One day as he sat in his fields reflecting upon his long life, he recalled a sermon he had heard in Dartmouth as a boy before he sailed to America. The horror of dying under the curse of God was impressed upon him as he meditated on the words he had heard so long ago and he was converted to Christ – eighty-five years after hearing John Flavel preach. Another remarkable convert was a London gentleman who tried to obtain some plays from a bookshop. The owner was a godly man and had none in stock but recommended Flavel's treatise *On Keeping the Heart*. The would-be reader scorned and threatened to burn the book but took it and returned in a month's time saying that God had used it to save his soul.

Flavel was a prolific writer and his works, separate and collected, have been republished many times since the author's lifetime. His complete works were republished in 1820 by W. Baynes & Son in London, making up six volumes. Although some of these writings are polemical, the author confessed that he found this kind of work disagreeable. His preference was for practical divinity, and it is here that his skill as a physician of souls shines most eminently. *Divine Conduct or the Mystery of Providence Opened* was first published in 1678 and has passed through several editions, the most recent being that published by the Sovereign Grace Union in 1935. The present edition differs from the original in two respects. Slight alterations of vocabulary and punctuation have been made, not to change, but to make clear the original force and sense of Flavel's words. Moreover, the treatise has been freshly subdivided and given new chapter headings. These are divisions which arise naturally out of the author's treatment of his subject. Thus, for all practical purposes, the matter of Flavel's work is unchanged, while the style of presentation has been altered slightly to help modern readers. This may have diminished the academic historical value of this edition, but it is hoped that it has greatly increased its spiritual usefulness to this generation.

Yet even granting the timeless spiritual value of John Flavel as a writer, some friends will deem it unwise to introduce him to the Christian public through his work on Providence. Surely it would be better to let an old writer speak on a subject that is not peculiar to his own era! Why not see what Flavel had to say on personal evangelism, on guidance or on the way to achieve peace and victory in the Christian life? These, without doubt, are the themes which popular preachers in our own day chiefly dwell upon. These are the topics about which most Christians wish to read. Why should we not, then, find out whether the Puritans really can help us on the burning issues of the day? In answer to this, there is no doubt that Flavel and his colleagues gave advice in these matters. But their whole approach was in marked contrast to that to which we are accustomed. Our modern piety, when it deals with spiritual problems, tends to be self-centred and subjective: 'How can I find peace? How can I be victorious and effective? How can I be guided?' If we know the answers to these questions, it is often felt, nothing more can be asked of us. Within the terms of such an outlook, little time and attention can be spared for the consideration of such an apparently theoretical subject as the Providence of God. It may even provoke some impatience. In view of the demands of modern life, is it really necessary for us to spend time reading a lengthy treatment of what is not a priority?

Flavel's approach to the subject of Providence cuts clean across our modern criticisms. He insists from the outset that it is the duty of believers to observe all the performances of God's providence for them, especially when they are in difficulties. Clearly, this conviction is not shared by the majority of evangelical Christians in the present day. It is not our custom nor is it regarded as a mark of spiritual keenness to seek to discover and meditate upon the work of Providence in all that happens to us. Two reasons for this may be suggested. First and foremost, the Puritans had a lively sense of the sovereignty of God and it is just this that, speaking generally, we lack today. Many Christians reject it intellectually as repugnant to free will and their understanding of the love of God. When they suffer a setback in their personal affairs or in the work of the gospel, it is ascribed wholly to the Devil or to failure in themselves to 'fulfil the conditions.' They feel a sense of personal frustration and may even believe that God Himself has been frustrated. Their only hope of success is to intensify their spiritual exercises. Prayer on this basis is not so much a plea to Omnipotence as the throwing of one's weight into the scale on the side of God. Even those who profess to accept without question the truth of divine sovereignty are not infrequently guilty of practical unbelief. Glibly to assert that 'all things work together for good to them that love God' is relatively easy, but to believe this when our circumstances are distasteful and appear likely to deteriorate is evidence of a spiritual apprehension of the sovereignty of God. Yet we cannot truly recognize and improve the workings of Providence until we learn from the Scriptures that God performs all things for us.

A second reason may be suggested why we do not meditate on the providence of God; it is that we have a deep distaste for meditation. This is not a matter of temperament. The recluse or introvert has no advantage over the active, busy Christian. True meditation is a work to which we are all naturally indisposed, but it is one to which the Holy Spirit prompts those whom He indwells, those who have trusted Christ. To the work of meditation upon Providence, believers must apply themselves; but first they must recognize it as a duty and understand what it involves.

When John Flavel writes of the Providence of God, he does not simply deliver a lecture. He writes in a thrilling way out of a full heart. He knows from Church history and from his own experience of the works of God on behalf of His people. Above all, he knows the Word of God intimately and he knows how to apply it. He shows how the hand of God may be discerned in our personal affairs, avoiding the extravagances of mysticism as well as the scepticism of unbelief. His treatise is calculated to abase man and exalt God, and yet to kindle faith and adoration in the heart of every child of God.

To learn of the Providence of God under the tuition of John Flavel will bring Christian believers into a sphere they never reckoned with before. It will also, we are confident, shed light on the great concerns of present-day evangelicals. How may we live a consecrated and victorious life? Let us first realize that everything does not depend on us. Let us see what God has done and is doing for our spiritual good. Then we may seek to work out what He is working in us. And what of guidance? Let us learn that, in an ultimate sense, we can never be 'outside of the will of God'. Flavel would teach us that God's will for us is our duty to be found in His Word. Moreover we should have a right attitude to all circumstances, even the most adverse. Finally, our Christian witness will not be crippled, as many fear, but quickened by a right apprehension of the sovereignty of God. What a great God is ours, greater than we ever thought when we first trusted Him for salvation! How futile for men and women to fight against Him! If Christians showed at all times by their demeanour that they had a living faith in the God of the Scriptures, they would be better placed to commend to an unbelieving world their God and His power to save.

MICHAEL BOLAND

February, 1963

INTRODUCTION

I will cry unto God most high; unto God that
performeth all things for me (Psalm 57. 2)

The greatness of God is a glorious and unsearchable mystery.
'For the Lord most high is terrible; he is a great king over all
the earth' (Ps. 47. 2). The condescension of the most high God
to men is also a profound mystery. 'Though the Lord be high,
yet hath he respect unto the lowly' (Ps. 138. 6). But when both
these meet together, as they do in this Scripture, they make up
a matchless mystery. Here we find the most high God per-
forming all things for a poor distressed creature.

It is the great support and solace of the saints in all the
distresses that befall them here, that there is a wise Spirit sitting in all the wheels of motion, and governing the most eccen-
tric creatures and their most pernicious designs to blessed and
happy issues. And, indeed, it were not worth while to live in a
world devoid of God and Providence.

How deeply we are concerned in this matter will appear by
that great instance which Psalm 57 presents us with. It was
composed, as the title notes, by David when he hid himself
from Saul in the cave. It is inscribed with a double title:
'Al-taschith, Michtam of David.' 'Al-taschith' refers to
the scope, and 'Michtam' to the dignity of the subject-
matter.

The former signifies 'destroy not,' or 'let there be no
slaughter,' and may either refer to Saul, concerning whom he
gave charge to his servants not to destroy him, or rather, it
has reference to God, to whom in this great exigency he

poured out his soul in this passionate ejaculation : 'Al-taschith,' 'destroy not.'

The latter title 'Michtam' signifies 'a golden ornament,' and so is suited to the choice and excellent matter of the Psalm, which much more deserves such a title than do Pythagoras' Golden Verses.

Three things are remarkable in the former part of the Psalm : his extreme danger; his earnest address to God in that extremity; and the arguments he pleads with God in that address.

His extreme danger is expressed in both the title and the body of the psalm. The title tells us this psalm was composed by him when he hid himself from Saul in the cave. This cave was in the wilderness of Engedi among the broken rocks where the wild goats lived, an obscure and desolate hole; yet even there the envy of Saul pursued him (1 Sam. 24. 1, 2). And now he that had been so long hunted as a partridge upon the mountains seems to be enclosed in the net. His enemies were outside the cave, from which there was no other outlet. Then Saul himself entered the mouth of this cave, in the sides and creeks of which David and his men lay hidden, and they actually saw him. Judge to how great an extremity and to what a desperate state things were now brought. Well might he say : 'My soul is among lions, and I lie even among them that are set on fire' (verse 4). What hope now remained? What but immediate destruction could be expected?

Yet this does not frighten him out of his faith and duty, but between the jaws of death he prays, and earnestly addresses himself to God for mercy : 'Be merciful unto me, O God, be merciful unto me' (verse 1). This excellent psalm was composed by him when there was enough to discompose the best man in the world. The repetition notes both the extremity of the danger and the ardency of the supplicant. Mercy, mercy, nothing but mercy, and that exerting itself in an extraordinary way, can now save him from ruin.

The arguments he pleads for obtaining mercy in this distress are very considerable. First, he pleads his reliance upon God as an argument to move mercy. 'Be merciful unto me, O God, be merciful unto me, for my soul trusteth in thee; yea, in the shadow of thy wings will I make my refuge, until these calamities be overpast' (verse 1). This his trust and dependence on God, though it is not an argument in respect of the dignity of the act, yet it is so in respect of the nature of the object, a compassionate God, who will not expose any that take shelter under His wings; also in respect of the promise by which protection is assured to them that fly to Him for sanctuary : 'Thou wilt keep him in perfect peace, whose mind is stayed on thee, because he trusteth in thee' (Isa. 26. 3). Thus he encourages himself from the consideration of that God in whom he trusts.

He pleads former experiences of His help in past distresses as an argument encouraging hope under the present strait : 'I will cry unto God most high, unto God that performeth all things for me' (verse 2).

In these words I shall consider two things : the duty resolved upon, and the encouragement to that resolution.

The duty resolved upon : 'I will cry unto God.' Crying unto God is an expression that denotes not only prayer, but intense and fervent prayer. To cry is to pray in a holy passion; and such are usually speeding prayers (Ps. 18. 6; Heb. 5. 7).

The encouragements to this resolution are taken from the sovereignty of God and from the experience he had of His Providence.

The sovereignty of God : 'I will cry unto God most high.' Upon this he acts his faith in extremity of danger. Saul is high, but God is the most high, and without His permission he is assured Saul cannot touch him. He had none to help, and if he had, he knew God must first help the helpers or they cannot help him. He had no means of defence or escape before him, but the Most High is not limited by means. This is a singular prop to faith (Ps. 59. 9).

The experience of His Providence hitherto : 'Unto God that performeth all things for me.'

The word which we translate 'performeth' comes from a root that signifies both to perfect, and to desist or cease. For when a business is performed and perfected, the agent then ceases and desists from working. To such a happy issue the Lord has brought all his doubtful and difficult matters before; and this gives him encouragement that He will still be gracious, and perfect that which concerns him now, as he speaks: 'The Lord will perfect that which concerneth me' (Ps. 138. 8).

The Septuagint renders Psalm 57. 2: 'The well-doer saving me,' 'who profits or benefits me.' And it is a certain truth that all the results and issues of Providence are profitable and beneficial to the saints. But the supplement in our translation well conveys the sense of the text: 'Who performeth all things.' And it involves the most strict and proper notion of Providence, which is nothing else but the performance of God's gracious purposes and promises to His people. And therefore Vatabulus and Muis supply and fill up the room left by the conciseness of the original with 'which he hath promised,' thus: 'I will cry unto God most high; unto God that performeth the things which he hath promised.' Payment is the performance of promises. Grace makes the promise, and Providence the payment.

Piscator fills it thus: 'unto God that performeth his kindness and mercy.' But still it supposes the mercy performed to be contained in the promise. Mercy is sweet in the promise, and much more so in the providential performance of it to us.

Castalio's supplement comes nearer to ours: 'I will cry unto God most high, unto God, the transactor of my affairs.'

But our English, making out the sense by a universal particle, is most agreeable to the scope of the text. For it cannot but be a great encouragement to his faith, that God had transacted all things, or performed all things for him. This Providence that never failed him in any of the straits that ever he met with (and his life was a life of many straits) he might well hope would not fail him now, though this were an extraordinary and matchless one.

Let us then bring our thoughts a little closer to this Scripture, and it will give us a fair and lovely prospect of Providence in its universal, effectual, beneficial and encouraging influence upon the affairs and concerns of the saints.

The expression imports the *universal* interest and influence of Providence in and upon all the concerns and interests of the saints. It not only has its hand in this or that, but in all that concerns them. It has its eye upon every thing that relates to them throughout their lives, from first to last. Not only the great and more important, but the most minute and ordinary affairs of our lives are transacted and managed by it. It touches all things that touch us, whether more nearly or remotely.

The text displays the *efficacy* of providential influences. Providence not only undertakes but perfects what concerns us. It goes through with its designs, and accomplishes what it begins. No difficulty so clogs it, no cross accident falls in its way, but it carries its design through it. Its motions are irresistible and uncontrollable; He performs it for us.

And (which is sweet to consider) all its products and issues are exceedingly *beneficial* to the saints. It performs all things for them. 'Tis true we often prejudge its works, and unjustly censure its designs, and in many of our straits and troubles we say: 'All these things are against us'; but indeed Providence neither does nor can do any thing that is really against the true interest and good of the saints. For what are the works of Providence but the execution of God's decree and the fulfilling of His Word? And there can be no more in Providence than is in them. Now there is nothing but good to the saints in God's purposes and promises; and, therefore, whatever Providence does concerning them, it must be (as the text speaks) 'the performance of all things for them.'

And if so, how *cheering, supporting and encouraging* must the consideration of these things be in a day of distress and trouble! What life and hope will it inspire our hearts and prayers with when great pressures lie upon us! It had such a cheering influence upon the Psalmist at this time, when the state of his affairs was, to the eye of sense and reason, forlorn and desperate; there was now but a hair's breadth (as we say) between him and ruin.

A powerful, enraged and implacable enemy had driven him into the hole of a rock, and was come after him into that hole.

Yet now, while his soul is among lions, while he lies in a cranny of the rock, expecting every moment to be drawn out to death, the reflections he had upon the gracious performances of the Most High for him, from the beginning to that moment, support his soul and inspire hope and life into his prayers : 'I will cry unto God most high, unto God that performeth all things for me.'

From the text then you have this doctrine : —

It is the duty of the saints, especially in times of straits, to reflect upon the performances of Providence for them in all the states and through all the stages of their lives.

The Church, in all the works of mercy, owns the hand of God : 'Lord, thou also hast wrought all our works in (or for) us' (Isa. 26. 12). And still it has been the pious and constant practice of the saints in all generations to preserve the memory of the more famous and remarkable providences that have befallen them in their times as a precious treasure. 'If thou be a Christian indeed, I know thou hast, if not in thy book, yet certainly in thy heart, a great many precious favours upon record; the very remembrance and rehearsal of them is sweet; how much more sweet was the actual enjoyment?'* Thus Moses, by divine direction, wrote a memorial of that victory obtained over Amalek as the fruit and return of prayer, and built there an altar with this inscription, *Jehovah-nissi* : 'The Lord my banner' (Exod. 17. 14, 15). Thus Mordecai and Esther took all care to perpetuate the memory of that signal deliverance from the plot of Haman, by ordaining the feast of Purim as an anniversary 'throughout every generation, every family, every province, and every city; that these days of Purim should not fail from among the Jews, nor the memorial of them perish from their seed' (Esther 9. 28). For this end you find Psalms indited, 'to bring to remembrance' (Ps. 70, title). You find parents giving suitable names to their children, that every time they looked upon them they might refresh the memory of

* Baxter's *Saints' Everlasting Rest.*

God's mercies (1 Sam. 1. 20). You find the very places where eminent providences have appeared, given a new name, for no other reason but to perpetuate the memorial of those sweet providences which so refreshed them there. Thus Bethel received its name (Gen. 28. 19). And that well of water where Hagar was seasonably refreshed by the angel in her distress, was called Beer-laha-roi: 'the well of him that liveth and looketh on me' (Gen. 16. 14). Yea, the saints have given, and God has assumed to Himself new titles upon this very score and account; Abraham's *Jehovah-jireh* and Gideon's *Jehovah-shalom* were ascribed to Him for this reason. And sometimes you find the Lord styles Himself 'The God that brought Abraham from Ur of the Chaldees' or 'The Lord God that brought them out of Egypt' or again 'The Lord that gathered them out of the north country'; reminding them of the gracious providences which in all those places He had wrought for them.

Now there is a twofold reflection upon the providential works of God.

One is entire and full, in its whole complex and perfect system. This blessed sight is reserved for the perfect state. It is in that mount of God where we shall see both the wilderness and Canaan, the glorious kingdom into which we are come, and the way through which we were led into it. There the saints shall have a ravishing view of it in its entirety, and every part shall be distinctly discerned, as it had its particular use, and as it was connected with the other parts, and how effectually and orderly they all wrought to bring about that blessed design of their salvation, according to the promise: 'And we know that all things work together for good to them that love God, to them who are the called according to his purpose' (Rom. 8. 28). For it is certain, no ship at sea keeps more exactly by the compass which directs its course, than Providence keeps by that promise which is its cynosure and pole-star.*

* 'When the records of eternity shall be exposed to view, all the counsels and results of that profound wisdom looked into; how will it transport when it shall be discerned: Lo, thus were the designs laid: here were the apt junctures and admirable dependencies of things, which, when acted upon the stage of time, seemed so perplexed and intricate.' (Howe, *Blessedness of the Righteous.*)

The other sight is partial and imperfect which we have on the way to glory, during which we only view it in its single acts, or at most, in some branches and more observable series of actions.

Between these two is the same difference as between the sight of the disjointed wheels and scattered pins of a watch, and the sight of the whole united in one frame and working in one orderly motion; or between an ignorant spectator who views some more observable vessel or joint of a dissected body, and the accurate anatomist who discerns the course of all the veins and arteries of the body as he follows the various branches of them through the whole, and plainly sees the proper place, figure and use of each, with their mutual respect to one another.

O how ravishing and delectable a sight will it be to behold at one view the whole design of Providence, and the proper place and use of every single act, which we could not understand in this world! What Christ said to Peter is as applicable to some providences in which we are now concerned as it was to that particular action : 'What I do, thou knowest not now; but thou shalt know hereafter' (John 13. 7). All the dark, intricate, puzzling providences at which we were sometimes so offended, and sometimes amazed, which we could neither reconcile with the promise nor with each other, nay, which we so unjustly censured and bitterly bewailed, as if they had fallen out quite against our happiness, we shall then see to be to us, as the difficult passage through the wilderness was to Israel, 'the right way to a city of habitation' (Ps. 107. 7).

And yet, though our present views and reflections upon Providence are so short and imperfect in comparison to that in heaven, yet such as it is under all its present disadvantages, it has so much excellence and sweetness in it that I may call it a little heaven, or as Jacob called his Bethel, 'the gate of heaven.' It is certainly a highway of walking with God in this world, and a soul may enjoy as sweet communion with Him in His providences as in any of His ordinances. How often have the hearts of its observers been melted into tears of joy at the beholding of its wise and unexpected productions! How often has it convinced them, upon a sober recollection of the events of their lives, that if the Lord had left them to their own counsels they had as often been their own tormenters, if not executioners! Into what and how many fatal mischiefs had they precipitated themselves if Providence had been as short-sighted as they! They have given it their hearty thanks for considering their interest more than their importunity, and not allowing them to perish by their own desires.

I

THE EVIDENCE OF
PROVIDENCE

I

THE WORK OF PROVIDENCE
FOR THE SAINTS

First, I shall undertake the proof and defence of the great truth that the affairs of the saints in this world are certainly conducted by the wisdom and care of special Providence. And in doing so I address myself with cheerfulness to perform, as I am able, a service for that Providence which has throughout my life 'performed all things for me,' as the text speaks.

There is a twofold consideration of Providence, according to its twofold object and manner of dispensation; the one in general, exercised about all creatures, rational and irrational, animate and inanimate; the other special and peculiar. Christ has a universal empire over all things (Eph. 1. 22); He is the head of the whole world by way of dominion, but a head to the Church by way of union and special influence (John 17. 2). He is 'the Saviour of all men, specially of those that believe' (1 Tim. 4. 10). The Church is His special care and charge. He rules the world for its good, as a head consulting the welfare of the body.

Heathens generally denied Providence, and no wonder, since they denied a God; for the same arguments that prove one will prove the other. Aristotle, the prince of heathen philosophers, could not by the utmost search of reason find out how the world originated, and therefore concludes it was from eternity. The Epicureans did, in a way, acknowledge a God, but yet denied a Providence, and wholly excluded Him from any interest or concern in the affairs of the world, as being inconsistent with the felicity and tranquillity of the divine Being, to be diverted and cumbered with the care and labour of government. This assertion is so repugnant to reason that it is a wonder they did not blush at its absurdity; but I guess the reason, and one of them (according to Cicero) speaks it out in broad language : *Itaque imposuistis cervicibus nostris sempiternum dominum, quem dies & noctes timeremus. Quis enim non timeat omnia providentem, & cogitantem, & animadvertentem, & omnia ad se pertinere putantem, curiosum & plenum negotii Deum?* (If this is so you have yoked us to an eternal master, such as we would fear day and night. For who would not be frightened of a prying busybody of a God who provides, plans and observes everything and who considers that everything is his concern?) They foresaw that the concession of a Providence would impose an eternal yoke upon their necks, by making them accountable for all they did to a higher tribunal, so that they must necessarily 'pass the time of their sojourning here in fear,' while all their thoughts, words and ways were strictly noted and recorded, for the purpose of an account by an all-seeing and righteous God. They therefore laboured to persuade themselves that what they had no mind for did not exist. But these atheistical and foolish conceits fall flat before the undeniable evidence of this so great and clear a truth.

Now my business here is not so much to deal with professed atheists who deny the existence of God and consequently deride all evidences brought from Scripture of the extraordinary events that fall out in favour of that people that are called His, but rather to convince those that professedly own all this, yet, never having tasted religion by experience, suspect, at least, that all these things which we call special providences to the saints, are but natural events or mere contingencies. Thus, while they profess to own a God and a Providence (which profession is but the effect of their education) they do in the meantime live like atheists, and both think and act as if there were no such things; and really, I fear this is the case with the greater part of the men of this generation.

But if it were indeed so, that the affairs of the world in

general, and more especially those of the saints, were not conducted by divine Providence, but, as they would persuade us, by the steady course of natural causes, beside which, if at any time we observe any event to fall out, it is merely casual and contingent, or proceeds from some hidden and secret cause in nature – if this indeed were so, let them that are tempted to believe it, give a rational answer to the following questions:

How comes it to pass that so many signal mercies and deliverances have befallen the people of God, above the power and against the course of natural causes, to make way for which there has been an obvious suspension and stop put to the course of nature?

It is most evident that no natural effect can exceed the power of its natural cause. Nothing can give to another more than it has in itself, and it is as clear that whatsoever acts naturally, acts necessarily. Fire burns to the uttermost of its power; while waters overflow and drown all that they can. Lions and other rapacious and cruel beasts, especially when hungry, tear and devour their prey; and arbitrary and rational agents also act according to the principles and laws of their natures. A wicked man when his heart is fully set in him, and his will stands in a full bent of resolution, will certainly, if he has power in his hand and opportunity to execute his conceived mischief, give it vent, and perpetrate the wicked devices of his heart. Having once conceived mischief, and 'travailing in pain with it,' according to the course of nature, he must 'bring it forth' (Ps. 7. 14). But if any of these inanimate, brute, or rational agents, when there is no natural obstacle or hindrance, have their power suspended, and that when the effect is near the birth and the design at the very point of execution, so that though they would, yet cannot hurt; to what, do you think, is this to be assigned and referred? Yet so it has often been seen, where God's interest has been immediately concerned in the danger and evil of the event The sea divided itself in its own channel, and made a wall of water on each side, to give God's distressed Israel a safe passage, and that not in a calm, but when its waves roared (Isa. 51. 15). The fire, when blown up to the most intense and vehement flame, had no power to singe one hair of God's faithful witnesses, when at the same instant it had power to destroy their intended executioners at a greater distance (Dan. 3. 22). Yea, we find it has sometimes been sufficient to consume, but not to torment the body, as in that known instance of blessed Bainham, who told his enemies: 'The flames were to him as a bed of roses.' The hungry lions put off their natural fierceness and became gentle and harmless when Daniel was cast among them for a prey. The like account we are given of Polycarp, and Dionysius the Areopagite, whom the fire would not touch, but stood after the manner of a shipman's sail filled with the wind about them.

Are these things according to the course and law of nature? To what secret natural cause can they be ascribed? In like manner we find the vilest and fiercest of wicked men have been withheld by an invisible hand of restraint from injuring the Lord's people. By what secret cause in nature was Jeroboam's hand dried up and made inflexible at the same instant it was stretched out against the man of God (1 Kings 13. 4)? No wild beasts rend and devour their prey more greedily than wicked men would destroy the people of God that dwell among them, were it not for this providential restraint upon them. So the Psalmist expresses his case in the words following my text: 'My soul is among lions, and I lie among them that are set on fire.' The disciples were sent forth 'as sheep into the midst of wolves' (Matt. 10. 16). It will not avail in this case to object that those miraculous events depend only upon Scripture testimony, which the atheist is not convinced by, for beside all that may be alleged for the authority of that testimony (which is needless to produce to men that own it), what is it less that every eye sees or may see at this day? Do we not behold a weak, defenceless handful of men wonderfully and otherwise unaccountably preserved from ruin in the midst of potent, enraged and turbulent enemies that fain would, but cannot, destroy them; when as yet no natural impediment can be assigned why they cannot?

And if this puzzle us, what shall we say when we see events produced in the world for the good of God's chosen, by those very hands and means which were intentionally employed for their ruin? These things are as much beside the intentions of their enemies as they are above their own expectations; yet such things are no rarities in the world. Was not the envy of Joseph's brethren, the cursed plot of Haman, and the decree procured by the envy of the princes against Daniel, with many more of the same kind, all turned by a secret and strange hand of Providence to their greater advancement and benefit? Their enemies lifted them up to all that honour and preferment they had.

How is it if the saints' affairs are not ordered by a special divine Providence that natural causes unite and associate themselves for their relief and benefit in so strange a manner as they are found to do?

It is undeniably evident that there are marvellous coincidences of Providence, confederating and agreeing, as it were, to meet and unite themselves to bring about the good of God's chosen. There is a similar face of things showing itself in several places at the same time, whenever any work for the good of the Church is come upon the stage of the world. As when the Messiah, the capital mercy, came to the temple, then Simeon and Anna were brought there by Providence as witnesses to it. So in Reformation work, when the images were pulled down in Holland, one and the same spirit of zeal possessed them in every city and town, that the work was done in a night. He that carefully reads the history of Joseph's advancement to be the lord of Egypt may number in that story twelve remarkable acts or steps of Providence by which he ascended to that honour and authority. If but one of them had failed, in all likelihood the event had done so too; but every one occurred in its order, exactly keeping its own time and place. So in the Church's deliverance from the plot of Haman, we find no less than seven acts of Providence concurring strangely to produce it, as if they had all met by appointment and consent to break that snare for them, one thing so aptly suiting with and making way for another that every careful observer must needs conclude that this cannot be the result of accident but wise counsel. Even as in viewing the accurate structure of the body of a man, the figure, position, and mutual relationships of the several members and vessels has convinced some, and is sufficient to convince all, that it is the work of divine wisdom and power; in like manner, if the admirable adaptation of the means and instruments employed for mercy to the people of God are carefully considered, who can but confess that as there are tools of all sorts and sizes in the shop of Providence, so there is a most skilful hand that uses them, and that they could no more produce such effects of themselves than the axe, saw, or chisel can cut or carve a rough log into a beautiful figure without the hand of a skilful artificer?

We find, by manifold instances, that there certainly are strong combinations and predispositions of persons and things to bring about some issue and design for the benefit of the Church, which they themselves never thought of. They hold no conference, they do not communicate their counsels to each other, yet meet together and work together as if they did, which is as if ten men should all meet together at one place, and in one hour, about one and the same business, and that without any previous appointment between themselves. Can any question that such a meeting of means and instruments is certainly, though secretly, overruled by some wise invisible agent?

If the concerns of God's people are not governed by a special Providence, how is it that the most apt and powerful means employed to destroy them are rendered ineffectual, while weak, contemptible means employed for their defence and comfort are crowned with success?

This could never be if things were wholly swayed by the course of nature. If we judge by that rule, we must conclude that the more apt and powerful the means are, the more successful and prosperous they must needs be; and where they are inept, weak, and contemptible, nothing can be expected of them. Thus reason lays it, according to the rules of nature, but Providence crosses its hands, as Jacob did in blessing the sons of Joseph, and orders quite contrary issues and events. Such was the mighty power and deep policy used by Pharaoh to destroy God's Israel, that to the eye of reason it was as impossible to survive it as for crackling thorns to abide unconsumed amidst devouring flames. By this emblem their miraculous preservation is expressed; the bush was all in a flame, but not consumed (Exod. 3. 2). The heathen Roman emperors, who made the world tremble and subdued the nations under them, employed all their power and policy against the poor, naked, defenceless Church, to ruin it, yet could not accomplish it (Rev. 12. 3, 4). O the seas of blood that heathen Rome shed in the ten persecutions! yet the Church lives. And when 'the dragon gave his power to the beast, (Rev. 13. 2) that is, the state of Rome became antichristian, O what slaughters were made by the beast in all his dominions, so that the Holy Ghost represents him as drunken with the blood of the saints (Rev. 17. 6). And yet all will not do; the gates, that is, the powers and policies of hell, cannot prevail against it. How manifest is the care and power of Providence herein! Had half that power been employed against any other people, it had certainly swallowed them up immediately, or, in the hundredth part of the time, worn them out. How soon was the Persian monarchy swallowed up by the Grecian, and that again by the Roman! Diocletian and Maximinus, in the height of their persecutions, found themselves so baffled by Providence that they both resigned the government and lived as private men. But in this wonderful preservation God makes good that promise: 'Though I make a full end of all nations, yet will I not make a full end of thee' (Jer. 30. 11), and 'No weapon formed against thee shall prosper' (Isa. 54. 17).

On the contrary, how successful have weak and contemptible means been made for the good of the Church! Thus in the first planting of Christianity in the world, by what weak and improbable instruments was it done! Christ did not choose the eloquent orators, or men of authority in the courts of kings and emperors, but twelve poor artisans and fishermen; and these not sent together in a troop, but some to take one country to conquer it, and some another. The most ridiculous course, in appearance, for such a design as could be imagined, and yet in how short a time was the Gospel spread and the Churches planted by them in the several kingdoms of the world! This the Psalmist foresaw by the Spirit of prophecy when he said: 'Out of the mouth of babes and sucklings hast thou ordained strength, to still the enemy and the avenger' (Ps. 8. 2). At the sound of rams' horns Jericho is delivered into the hands of Israel (Josh. 6. 20). By three hundred men, with their pitchers and lamps, the huge host of Midian is discomfited (Judges 6. 19). The Protestants besieged in Beziers in France are delivered by a drunken drummer who, going to his quarters at midnight, rang the alarm-bell of the town, not knowing what he did; and just then their enemies were making their assault. And as weak and improbable means have been blessed with success to the Church in general, so to the preservation of its particular members also. A spider, by weaving her web over the mouth of an oven, shall hide a servant of Christ, Du Moulin, from his enemies, who took refuge there in that bloody Parisian massacre. A hen shall sustain another many days at the same time by lodging her egg every day in the place where he had hid himself from the cut-throats. Examples might be easily multiplied, but the truth is too plain and obvious to the observation of all ages to need them. And can we but acknowledge a divine and special Providence overruling these matters, when we see the most apt and potent means for the Church's ruin frustrated, and the most silly and contemptible means granted success and prospered for its good?

If all things are governed by the course of nature and force of natural causes, how then comes it to pass that, like a bowl

when it strikes another, men are turned out of the way of
evil, along which they were driving at full speed?

Good men have been going along the way to their own
ruin, and did not know it; but Providence has met them in the
way and preserved them by strange diversions, the meaning
of which they did not understand till the event revealed it.
When Paul lay bound at Cæsarea, the high priest and chief of
the Jews request Festus that he might be brought bound to
Jerusalem, having laid wait in the way to kill him; but Festus,
though ignorant of the plot, utterly refuses it, and chooses
rather to go with them to Cæsarea and judge him there. By this
diversion their bloody design is frustrated (Acts 25. 3, 4).

Possidonius, in the life of Augustine, tells us that the good
father, going to teach the people of a certain town, took a
guide with him to show him the way. The guide mistook the
usual road and unwittingly took a by-path, by which means
Augustine escaped ruin by the hands of the bloody Donatists
who, knowing his intention, waylaid him to kill him on the
road.

And as memorable and wonderful are those rubs and diversions wicked men have met with in the way of perpetrating
the evils conceived and intended in their own hearts. Laban
and Esau came against Jacob with mischievous purposes, but
no sooner are they come near him but the shackles of restraint
are immediately clapped upon them both, so that their hands
cannot perform their enterprises. Balaam runs greedily, for
reward, to curse Israel, but meets with an unexpected check at
his very outset; and though that did not stop him, he tried
every way to do them mischief, yet he still finds himself fettered by an effectual bond of restraint that he can in no way
shake off (Num. 22. 25, 38). Saul, the high priest's bloodhound,
breathes out threatenings against the Church, and goes with a
bloody commission towards Damascus, to hale the poor flock
of Christ to the slaughter; but when he comes near the place
he meets an unexpected stop on the way, by which the mischief is not only diverted, but he himself is converted to

Christ (Acts 9. 1–4). Who can fail to see the finger of God in these things!

If there is not an over-ruling Providence ordering all things for the good of God's people, how comes it to pass that the good and evil which is done to them in this world is accordingly repaid into the bosoms of them that are instrumental therein?

How clear is it to every man's observation, that the kindnesses and benefits any have done to the Lord's people have been rewarded with full measure into their bosoms! The Egyptian midwives refused to obey Pharaoh's inhuman command, and saved the male children of Israel; for this 'the Lord dealt well with them and built them houses' (Exod. 1. 21). The Shunammite was hospitable and careful for Elisha, and God recompensed it with the desirable enjoyment of a son (2 Kings 4. 9, 17). Rahab hid the spies, and was exempted from the destruction of Jericho (Heb. 11. 31). Publius, the chief man of the island of Melita, courteously received and lodged Paul after his shipwreck; the Lord speedily repaid him for that kindness, and healed his father, who lay sick at that time of a bloody flux and fever (Acts 28. 7, 8).

In like manner, we find the evils done to God's people have been repaid by a just retribution to their enemies. Pharaoh and the Egyptians were cruel enemies to God's Israel, and designed the ruin of their poor innocent babes; and God repaid it in smiting all the first-born of Egypt in one night (Exod. 12. 29). Haman erected a gallows fifty cubits high for good Mordecai, and God so ordered it that he himself and his ten sons were hanged on it. And indeed it was but meet that he should eat the fruit of that tree which he himself had planted (Esther 7. 10). Ahithophel plots against David, and gives counsel like an oracle how to procure his fall; and that very counsel, like an overcharged gun, recoils upon himself, and procures his ruin. Seeing his good counsel rejected (good politically, not morally), it was now easy for him to guess the outcome, and so his own fate (2 Sam. 17. 23).

Charles IX most inhumanly made the very canals of Paris flow with Protestant blood, and soon after he died miserably, his blood flowing from all parts of his body. Stephen Gardiner, who burnt so many of God's dear servants to ashes, was himself so scorched up by a terrible inflammation that his very tongue was black and hung out of his mouth, and in dreadful torments he ended his wretched days. Maximinus, that cruel emperor, who set forth his proclamation engraven in brass for the utter abolishing of the Christian religion, was speedily smitten like Herod with a dreadful judgment, swarms of lice preying upon his entrails, and causing such a stench that his physicians could not endure to come near him, and for refusing to do so were slain. Hundreds of like instances might easily be produced to confirm this observation. And who can but see by these things that 'verily there is a God that judgeth in the earth!'

Yea, so exact have been the retributions of Providence to the enemies of the Church, that not only the same persons, but the same members, that have been the instruments of mischief, have been made the subjects of wrath. The same arm which Jeroboam stretched out to smite the prophet, God smites. The emperor Aurelian, when he was ready to subscribe the edict for the persecution of the Christians, was suddenly cramped in his knuckles that he could not write. Greenhill, in his exposition upon Ezekiel 11. 13, tells his hearers that there was one then present in the congregation who was an eye-witness of a woman scoffing at another for purity and holy walking, who had her tongue stricken immediately with the palsy, and died of it within two days. Henry II of France, in a great rage against a Protestant counsellor, committed him to the hands of one of his nobles to be imprisoned, and that with these words, that 'he would see him burned with his own eyes.' But, mark the righteous providence of God, within a few days after, the same nobleman, with a lance put into his hands by the king, did at a tilting match run the said king into one of his eyes, from which he died.

Yea, Providence has made the very place of sinning the place of punishment: 'In the place where dogs licked the blood of Naboth, shall dogs lick thy blood' (1 Kings 21. 19); and it was exactly fulfilled (2 Kings 9. 26). Thus Tophet is made a burying-place for the Jews, till there was no room to bury; and that was the place where they had offered up their sons to Moloch (Jer. 7. 31, 32). The story of Nightingale is generally known, which Foxe relates, how he fell out of the pulpit and broke his neck, while he was abusing that Scripture (1 John 1. 10). And thus the Scriptures are made good by Providence. 'Whoso diggeth a pit shall fall therein; and he that rolleth a stone, it shall return upon him' (Prov. 26. 27), and 'with what measure ye mete, it shall be measured to you again' (Matt. 7. 2).

If any shall still say that these things may fall out accidentally, and that many thousands of the Church's enemies have died in peace, and their end been like other men, we answer with Augustine: 'If no sin were punished here, no Providence would be believed; and if every sin should be punished here, no judgment would be expected.' But, that none may think these events to be merely casual and accidental, we shall enquire yet further.

If these things are merely accidental, how is it that they square and agree so exactly with the Scriptures in all particulars?

We read: 'Can two walk together except they be agreed?' (Amos 3. 3). If two men travel along one road, it is likely they are agreed to go to the same place. Providences and Scriptures go all one way, and if they seem at any time to go different or opposite ways, be sure they will meet at the journey's end. There is an agreement between them so to do.

Does God miraculously suspend the power of natural causes? Why, this is no accidental thing, but what harmonizes with the Word 'When thou passest through the waters, I will be with thee, and through the rivers, they shall not overflow thee. When thou walkest through the fire, thou shalt not be burned, neither shall the flame kindle upon thee' (Isa. 43. 2).

Do natural causes unite and associate themselves for the

good of God's people? Why, this is no more than what is contained in the promises, and is but the fulfilling of that Scripture: 'All is yours, for ye are Christ's' (1 Cor. 3. 22); that is, the use, benefit and service of all the creatures is for you, as your need shall require.

Are the most apt and powerful means employed for their ruin frustrated? Who can but see the Scriptures fulfilled in, and expounded by such providences (*see* Isa. 8. 8–10; 54. 15–17; expounded by 2 Kings 18. 17, etc.)!

Do you see at any time a rub of Providence diverting the course of good men from falling into evil, or wicked men from committing evil? How loudly do such Providences proclaim the truth and certainty of the Scriptures, which tell us that 'the way of man is not in himself, neither is it in him that walketh to direct his steps' (Jer. 10. 23), and that 'a man's heart deviseth his way: but the Lord directeth his steps' (Prov. 16. 9)!

Do you see adequate retributions made to those that injure or befriend the people of God? Why, when you see all the kindness and love they have shown the saints returned with interest into their bosoms, how is it possible but you must see the accomplishment of these Scriptures in such providences! 'But the liberal soul deviseth liberal things, and by liberal things he shall stand' (Isa. 32. 8; 2 Cor. 9. 6).

And when you see the evils men have done, or intended to do to the Lord's people, recoiling upon themselves, he is perfectly blind that does not see the harmony such providences bear with such Scriptures as Psalm 7. 14–16; 9. 16; and 140. 11, 12.

O what exact proportions do providences and Scriptures hold! Little do men take notice of it. Why did Cyrus, contrary to all rules of state policy, freely dismiss the captives, except to fulfil the Scripture (Isa. 45. 13)? So that it was well observed by one that, 'as God hath stretched out the expansum or firmament over the natural; so he hath stretched out his Word over the rational world.' And as the creatures on earth are influenced by those heavenly bodies, so are all creatures in the world influenced by the Word, and do infallibly fulfil it, when they design to thwart it.

If these things are contingent, how is it that they fall out so remarkably in the nick of time, which makes them so greatly observable to all that consider them?

We find a multitude of providences so timed to a minute, that had they occurred just a little sooner or later, they had mattered little in comparison with what now they do. Certainly, it cannot be chance, but counsel, that so exactly works in time. Contingencies keep to no rules.

How remarkable to this purpose were the tidings brought to Saul, that 'the Philistines have invaded the land' (1 Sam. 23. 27), just as he was ready to grasp the prey! The angel calls to Abraham, and shows him another sacrifice just when his hand was giving the fatal stroke to Isaac (Gen. 22. 10, 11). A well of water is shown to Hagar just when she had left the child, as not able to see its death (Gen. 21. 16, 19). Rabshakeh meets with a blasting providence, hears a rumour that frustrated his design, just when ready to make an assault upon Jerusalem (Isa. 37. 7, 8). So when Haman's plot against the Jews was ripe, and all things ready for execution, 'on that night could not the king sleep' (Esth. 6. 1). When the horns are ready to gore Judah, immediately carpenters are prepared to fray them away (Zech. 1. 18–21).

How remarkable was the relief of La Rochelle by a shoal of fish that came into the harbour when they were ready to perish with famine, such as they never observed before, nor after that time! Mr Dod could not go to bed one night, but has a strong impulse to visit, though unseasonably, a neighbour gentleman, and just as he came there, he meets him at his door, with a halter in his pocket, just going to hang himself. Dr Tate and his wife, in the Irish rebellion, were flying through the woods with a sucking-child, which was just ready to expire. The mother going to rest it upon a rock, puts her hand upon a bottle of warm milk, by which it was preserved. A good woman, from whose mouth I received it, being driven to a great extremity, all supplies failing, was exceedingly plunged into unbelieving doubts and fears, not seeing where supplies should come from; when, lo! in the nick of time, turning over some things in a chest, unexpectedly she lights upon a piece of gold, which supplied her present needs till God opened another door of supply. If these things fall out by accident, how is it they come in the very nick of time so exactly, as that it is become proverbial in Scripture, 'In the mount of the Lord it shall be seen' (Gen. 22. 14)?

Lastly, were these things accidental and contingent, how can it be that they should fall out so immediately upon and consonantly to the prayers of the saints? So that in many providences they are able to discern a very clear answer to their prayers, and are sure they have the petitions they asked (1 John 5. 15).

Thus the sea divided itself just at the time of Israel's cry to heaven (Exod. 14. 10). So signal a victory is given to Asa immediately at the time of that passionate cry to heaven : 'Help us, O Lord our God' (2 Chron. 14. 11, 12). Ahithophel goes and hangs himself, just at the time of that prayer of distressed David (2 Sam. 15. 31). Haman falls and his plot is broken, just at the time of the fast kept by Mordecai and Esther (Esth. 4. 16). Our own Speed, in his History of Britain, tells us that Richard I besieged a castle with his army; they offered to surrender if he would save their lives; he refuses, and threatens to hang them all. Upon this an arbalester* charged his bow with a square arrow, making first his prayer to God that he would direct the shot and deliver the innocent from oppression; it struck the king himself, from which he died, and they were delivered. Abraham's servant prayed for success; and see how it was answered (Gen. 24. 45). Peter was cast into prison, and prayer was made for him by the Church, and see the event (Acts 12. 5, 6, 7, 12). I could easily add to these the wonderful examples of the return of prayers which was observed in Luther, and Dr Winter in Ireland, and many more; but I judge

* Crossbow-man.

it needless because most Christians have a stock of experience of their own, and are well assured that many of the providences that befall them are, and can be no other than the return of their prayers.

And now who can be dissatisfied in this point that wisely considers these things? Must we not conclude that 'he withdraweth not his eyes from the righteous' (Job 36. 7) and that 'The eyes of the Lord run to and fro throughout the whole earth, to show himself strong in the behalf of them whose heart is perfect towards him' (2 Chron. 16. 9). His providences proclaim Him to be a God who hears prayer.

2

OUR BIRTH AND UPBRINGING

═══

Having proved that the affairs of the saints in this world are certainly conducted by the wisdom and care of a special Providence, my next work is to show you in what affairs and concerns of theirs the Providence of God more especially appears, or what are the most remarkable performances of Providence for them in this world.

And here I am not led directly by my text to speak of the most internal and spiritual performances of Providence immediately relating to the souls of His people, though they all relate to their souls mediately and eventually, but of the more visible and external performances of Providence for them. It is not to be supposed that I should touch all these – they are more than the sands – but what I aim at is to discourse to you on some more special and more observable performances of Providence for you.

To start with, let us consider how well Providence has performed the first work that ever it did for us: *in our formation and protection in the womb*. Certainly this is a very glorious and admirable performance; it is that which the Psalmist admires: 'My substance was not hid from thee, when I was made in secret, and curiously wrought in the lowest parts of the earth' (139. 15). The womb is so called for this reason, that as skilful artists, when they have some choice piece in hand, perfect it in private, and then bring it into the light for all to gaze at; so it was here. Two things are admirable in this performance of Providence for us.

First, the rare structure and excellent composition of the body. 'I am wonderfully made'; that word *ruchampti* is very full. The vulgate renders it, 'painted as with a needle,' i.e., richly embroidered with nerves and veins. O, the skilful workmanship that is in that one part, the eye! How has it forced some to acknowledge a God upon the examination of it! Providence, when it went about this work, had its model or pattern before it, according to which it moulded every part, 'In thy book all my members were written' (verse 16). Have you an integral perfection and fulness of members? It is because He wrote them all in His book, or painted your body according to that exact model which He drew of you in His own gracious purpose before you had a being. Had an eye, an ear, a hand, a foot been wanting in the plan, you had now been sadly aware of the defect. This world had been but a dungeon to you without those windows, and you had lived, as many do, an object of pity to others. If you have low thoughts of this mercy, ask the blind, the deaf, the lame and the dumb, the value and worth of those mercies, and they will tell you. There is a world of cost bestowed upon your very body. You might have been cast into another mould, and created a worm or a toad. I remember Luther tells us of two cardinals riding in great pomp to the Council of Constance, and by the way they heard a man in the fields bitterly weeping and wailing. When they came to him they found him intently viewing an ugly toad; and asking him why he wept so bitterly, he told them his heart was melted with this consideration, that God had not made him such a loathsome and deformed creature. 'This is what I love to weep at,' said he; whereupon one of them cries out: well said the father, 'The unlearned will rise and take heaven, and we with all our learning shall be cast into hell.' No part of the common lump was so figured and polished as man is. Galen gave Epicurus a hundred years to imagine a more commodious situation, configuration or composition of any one member of a human body. And if all the angels had studied to this day, they could not have cast the body of man into a better mould.

And yet all this is but the enamelling of the case, or polishing the casket in which the rare jewel lies. Providence has not only built the house, but brought the inhabitant (I mean the soul) into the possession of it. A glorious piece it is, that bears the very image of God upon it, being all in all, and all in every part. How noble are its faculties and affections! How nimble, various and indefatigable are its motions! How comprehensive is its capacity! It is a companion for angels, nay, capable of espousal to Christ and eternal communion with God. It is the wonder of earth, and the envy of hell.

Suppose now (and why should you not suppose what you so frequently behold in the world?) that Providence had so permitted and ordered it, that your soul had entered into your body with one or two of its faculties wounded and defective. Suppose its understanding had been cracked; what a miserable life you would have lived in this world, being capable of neither service nor comfort. And truly, when I have considered those works of Providence, in bringing into the world in all countries and ages some such spectacles of pity; some deprived of the use of reason and differing from beasts in little more than shape and figure; and others, though sound in their under-standings, yet deformed or defective in their bodies, monstrous, mis-shapen and loathsome creatures; I can resolve the design of this Providence into nothing else but a demonstration of His sovereign power; unless they are designed as foils to set off the beauty of other rare and exquisite pieces, and intended to stand before your eyes as monitors of God's mercy to you, that your hearts, as often as you behold them, might be melted into thankfulness for distinguishing favour to you.

Look then, but not proudly, upon your outside and inside. See and admire what Providence has done for you, and how well it has performed the first service that ever it did for you in this world. And yet, this was not all it did for you. Before you saw this world, it preserved you, as well as formed you in the womb, else you had been as those embryos Job speaks of 'which never saw light' (3. 16). Abortives go for nothing in the world, and there are multitudes of them. Some never had a reasonable soul breathed into them, but only the rudiments and rough draft of a body; these come not into the account of men, but perish as the beast does. Others die in, or shortly after they come out of the womb, and though their life was but a moment, yet that moment entails an eternity upon them. Had this been your case, as it is the case of millions, then, supposing your salvation, yet you had been utterly unserviceable to God in the world; none had been the better for you, nor you the better for any in the world. You had been utterly incapable of all that good which throughout your life you have either done to others or received from others.

And if we consider the nature of that obscure life we lived in the womb, how small an accident, had it been permitted by Providence, could have extinguished our life, like a bird in the shell? We cannot therefore but admire the tender care of Providence over us, and say with the Psalmist: 'Thou hast covered me in my mother's womb' (139. 13): and not only so, 'But thou art he that took me out of the womb' (22. 9). He preserved you there to the fulness of time and, when that time was come, brought you safely through manifold hazards into that place in the world which He from eternity prepared for you.

Another great performance of Providence for the people of God respects *the place and time of their birth*. And truly, this is no small concern to every one of us, but of vast consequence, either to our good or evil, though it is little considered by most men. I am persuaded the thoughts of few Christians penetrate deep enough into this Providence, but slide too slightly and superficially over an abyss of much mercy, rich and manifold mercy wrapped up in this gracious performance of Providence for them.

Ah friends! can you think it an indifferent thing into what part of the world the womb of nature has cast you out? Does nothing depend upon what spot of the creation, or in what age of the world, your lot has fallen? It may be you have not seriously thought about this matter. And because this point is so seldom touched, I will therefore dive a little more particularly and distinctly into it, and endeavour to warm your affections with a representation of the many and rich benefits you owe to this one performance of Providence for you.

We will consider it under a double respect or relation, as it respects your present comfort in this world, and as it relates to your eternal happiness in the world to come.

This performance of Providence for you very much concerns your present comfort in this world. All the rooms in this great house are not alike pleasant and commodious for the inhabitants of it. You read of 'the dark places of the earth,' which 'are full of the habitations of cruelty' (Ps. 74. 20); and many such dismal places are found in the habitable earth. What a vast tract of the world lies as a waste wilderness!

Suppose your mothers had brought you forth in America, among the savage Indians, who herd together as brute beasts, are scorched with heat, and starved with cold, being naked, destitute and defenceless. How poor, miserable, and unprovided with earthly comfort and accommodations are many millions of the inhabitants of this world! What mercies do you enjoy in respect of the amenity, fertility, temperature, and civility of the place of your habitation? What is it but a garden enclosed out of a wilderness? I may without partiality or vanity say, God has, even upon temporal accounts, provided you with one of the healthiest, pleasantest, and in all respects the best furnished room in all the great house of this world. Hear what our own chronicler says of it: 'It is the fortunate island, the paradise of pleasure, the garden of God; whose valleys are like Eden, whose hills are as Lebanon, whose springs are as Pisgah, whose rivers are as Jordan, whose wall is the ocean, and whose defence is the Lord Jehovah.'

You are here provided with necessary and comfortable accommodations for your bodies, that a great part of the world are unacquainted with. It is not with the poorest among us, as it is said to be with the poor Russians, whose poverty pinches and bites with such sharp teeth that their poor cry at the doors: 'Give me and cut me! give me and kill me!'

Do not say that the barbarous nations excel you in that they possess the mines of silver and gold, which it may be you think enough to make up for all other inconveniences of life. Alas, poor creatures! better had it been for them if their country had brought forth briars and thorns, instead of gold, silver, and precious stones; for this has been the occasion of ruining all their other comforts in this world, this has invited their cruel avaricious enemies among them, under whose servitude they groan and die without mercy, and thousands of them have chosen death rather than life on the terms they enjoyed it. And why might not your lot have fallen there as well as where it is? Are not they made of the same clay and endowed with as good a nature as yourselves? O what a distinction has divine mercy made, where nature made none! Consider, ungrateful man, you might have fallen into some of those regions where a tainted air frequently cloys the jaws of death, where the inhabitants differ very little from the beasts in the manner of their living; but God has provided for you, and given the poorest among us far better accommodations of life than the greatest among them are ordinarily provided with. O what Providence has done for you!

But all that I have said is very inconsiderable in comparison with the spiritual mercies and advantages you here enjoy for your souls. O this is such an advantageous cast of Providence for you as obliges you to a thankful acknowledgment of it to all eternity. For let us here make but a few suppositions in the case before us, and the glory of Providence will shine like a sunbeam full in your faces.

Suppose it had been your lot to have fallen in any of those vast continents possessed by pagans and heathens at this day, who bow down to the stock of a tree, and worship the host of heaven. This is the case of millions, and millions of millions, for pagan idolaters, as that searching scholar, Brerewood, informs us, do not only fill the circumference of nine hundred miles in Europe, but almost the one half of Africa, more than the half of Asia, and almost the whole of America.

O how deplorable had your case been if a pagan idolatress had brought you forth, and idolatry had been sucked in with your mother's milk! Then, in all probability, you had been at this day worshipping devils, and racing at full speed in the direct road to damnation, for these are the people of God's wrath: 'Pour out thy fury upon the heathen that know thee not, and upon the families that call not upon thy name' (Jer. 10. 25). How dreadful is that imprecation against them, which takes hold of them and all that is theirs! 'Confounded be all they that serve graven images, that boast themselves of idols' (Ps. 97. 7).

Or suppose your lot had fallen among Mahometans, who next to pagans spread over the greatest tract of the earth, for though Arabia bred that unclean bird, yet that cage could not long contain him; for not only the Arabians, but the Persians, Turks, and Tartars, do all bow down their backs under that grand impostor. This poison has dispersed itself through the veins of Asia, over a great part of Africa, even the circumference of seven thousand miles, and does not stop there, but has tainted a considerable part of Europe also.

Had your lot fallen here, O what unhappy men and women had you been, notwithstanding the natural amenity and pleasantness of your native soil! You had then adored a grand imposter, and died in a fool's paradise. Instead of God's living oracles, you had been, as they now are, deceived to your eternal ruin with such fond, mad and wild dreams, as whoso considers would think the authors had more need of manacles and fetters than arguments or sober answers.

Or if neither of these had been your lot, suppose you had been emptied by the womb of nature into this little spot of the earth which is Christianized by profession, but nevertheless for the most part overrun by popish idolatry and anti-christian delusions. What unhappy men and women had you been had you sucked a Popish breast! for his people are to be the subjects of the vials of God's wrath to be poured out successively upon them (Rev. 16), and the Scriptures in round and plain language tell us what their fate must be: 'And for this cause God shall send them strong delusion, that they should believe a lie, that they all might be damned who believed not the truth, but had pleasure in unrighteousness' (2 Thess. 2. 11, 12).

Nay, you might have fallen into the same land in which your habitation now is, and yet have had no advantage by it as to salvation, if He that chose the bounds of your habitation had not also graciously 'determined the times' for you (Acts 17. 26).

Suppose your lot had fallen where it is, during the pagan state of England, where for many hundred years were gross and vile idolators. Thick darkness overspread the people of this island and, as in other countries, the devil was worshipped, and his lying oracles zealously believed.

The shaking of the top of Jupiter's oak in Dodona, the cauldron smitten with the rod in the hand of Jupiter's image, the laurel and fountain in Daphne : these were the ordinances on which the poor, deluded wretches waited. So in this nation they worshipped idols also. The sun and moon were adored for gods, together with many abominable idols which our ancestors worshipped and whose memorials are not to this day quite obliterated among us.

Or suppose our lot had fallen in those later miserable days in which Queen Mary sent so many hundreds to heaven in a fiery chariot, when the poor Protestants skulked up and down in holes and woods to preserve themselves from popish inquisitors, who, like blood-hounds, hunted up and down through all the cities, towns and villages of the nation, to seek out the poor sheep of Christ for a prey.

But such has been the special care of Providence towards us, that our turn to be brought upon the stage of this world was graciously reserved for better days, so that if we had had our own option, we could not have chosen for ourselves as Providence has done. We are not only furnished with the best room in this great house, but before we were put into it, it was swept with the broom of national Reformation from idolatry, yea, and washed by the blood of martyrs from popish filthiness, and adorned with Gospel lights, shining in as great lustre in our days, as ever they did since the apostles' days. You might have been born in England for many ages, and not have found a Christian in it; yea, and since Christianity was here owned, and not have met a Protestant in it. O what an obligation has Providence laid you under, by such a merciful performance as this for you!

If you say: 'All this indeed is true, but what is this to eternal salvation? Do not multitudes that enjoy these privileges eternally perish notwithstanding them; yea, and perish with an aggravation of sin and misery beyond other sinners?'

True, they do so, and it is very sad that it should be so; but yet we cannot deny this to be a very choice and singular mercy, to be born in such a land, and at such a time. For let us consider what helps for salvation men here enjoy, beyond what they could enjoy had their lot fallen according to the forementioned suppositions.

Here we enjoy the ordinary means of salvation, which elsewhere men are denied and cut off from. So that if any among the heathen are saved and brought to Christ, it must be in some miraculous or extraordinary way, for 'how shall they believe in him of whom they have not heard, and how shall they hear without a preacher?' (Rom. 10. 14). Alas! were there a desire awakened in any of their hearts after a Gospel-discovery of salvation, which ordinarily is not nor can be rationally supposed, yet, poor creatures, they might travel from sea to sea to hear the Word, and not find it; whereas you can hardly miss the opportunities of hearing the Gospel. Sermons meet you frequently, so that you can scarcely shun or avoid the ordinances and instruments of your salvation. And is this nothing? Christ even forces Himself upon us.

Here, in this age of the world, the common prejudices against Christianity are removed by the advantage it has of a public profession among the people, and protection by the laws of the country. Whereas were your habitation among Jews, Mahometans, or heathen idolaters, you would find Christ and Christianity the common odium of the country, every one defying and deriding both name and thing, and such yourselves likely had been, if your birth and education had been among them. For you may observe that whatever is traditionally delivered down from father to son, every one is fond of and zealous in its defence. The Jews, heathens and Mahometans are at this day so tenacious of their errors that, with spitting, hissing, and clapping of hands, and all other signs of indignation and abhorrence, they chase away all others from among them.

Is it not then a special mercy to you to be cast into such a country and age, where, as a learned divine observes, the true religion has the same advantages over every false one, as in other countries they have over it? Here you have the presence of precious means, and the absence of soul-destroying prejudices—two signal mercies.

Here, in this age of the world, Christianity confronts you as soon as you are capable of any sense or impressions of religion upon you; and so, by an happy anticipation, blocks up the passages by which a false religion would else certainly enter. Here you suck in the first notions and principles of Christianity, even with the mother's milk, and certainly such a prepossession is a choice advantage. *Quo semel est imbuta, recens servabit odorem testa diu.* (For many a day the pot will keep the scent of that which first it held, when freshly baked.) 'Train up a child in the way he should go; and when he is old, he will not depart from it' (Prov. 22. 6).

Here you have, or may have, the help and assistance of Christians to direct your way, resolve your doubts, support your burdens and help you through those difficulties that attend the new birth. Alas! if a poor soul had any beginnings or faint workings and stirrings after Christ and true religion in many other countries, the hand of every man would presently be against him, and none would be found to relieve, assist or encourage, as you may see in that example of Galeacius. The nearest relations would, in that case, prove the greatest enemies, the country would quickly hoot at him as a monster and cry: 'Away with the heretic to the prison or stake.'

Whether these eventually prove blessings to your souls or

not, certain I am that in themselves they are singular mercies, and helps to salvation that are denied to millions besides you. So that if Plato when he was near his death could bless God for three things, *viz.*, that he was a man and not a beast, that he was born in Greece, and that he was brought up in the time of Socrates, much more cause have you to admire Providence, that you are men and not beasts; that you were born in England, and that you are brought up in Gospel days. This is a land the Lord has espied for you, as the expression is (Ezek. 20. 6), and concerning it you have abundant cause to say, as in another case the Psalmist does: 'The lines are fallen unto me in pleasant places; yea, I have a goodly heritage' (16. 6).

Another performance of Providence which must be carefully noticed and weighed is *the designation of the stock and family out of which we should spring and rise*. And truly this is of special consideration, both as to our temporal and eternal good. For whether the families in which we grew up were great or small in Israel, whether our parents were of the higher or lower class and rank among men, yet if they were such as feared God and wrought righteousness, if they took any care to educate you religiously and train you up 'in the nurture and admonition of the Lord,' you are bound to reckon it among your chief mercies, that you sprang from the loins of such parents, for from this spring a double stream of mercy rises to you.

First, temporal and external mercies to your outward man. You cannot but know that as godliness entails a blessing, so wickedness and unrighteousness a curse upon posterity. An instance of the former you have in Genesis 17. 18–20; on the contrary you have the threatening, Zechariah 5. 4, and both together in this passage: 'The curse of the Lord is in the house of the wicked; but he blesseth the habitation of the just' (Prov. 3. 33). True it is that both these imply the children's treading in the steps of their parents (Ezek. 18), but how frequently is it seen that wicked men breed their children vainly and wickedly; so that as it is said of Abijam: 'and he walked in all the sins of his father, which he had done before him' (1 Kings 15. 3); and so the curse is entailed from generation to generation. To escape this curse is a choice providence.

But especially take notice what a stream of spiritual blessings and mercies flows from this Providence to the inner man. O, it is no common mercy to descend from pious parents. Some of us do not only owe our natural life to them, as instruments of our beings, but our spiritual and eternal life also. It was no small mercy to Timothy to be descended from such progenitors (2 Tim. 1. 5), nor to Augustine that he had such a mother as Monica, who planted in his mind the precepts of life with her words, watered them with her tears, and nourished them with her example. We will a little more particularly inspect this mercy, and in so doing we shall find manifold mercies contained in it.

What a mercy was it to us to have parents that prayed for us before they had us, as well as in our infancy, when we could not pray for ourselves? Thus did Abraham (Gen. 15. 2) and Hannah (1 Sam. 1. 10, 11), and probably some here are the fruits and returns of their parents' prayers. This was that holy course they continued all their days for you, carrying all your concerns, especially your eternal ones, before the Lord with their own; and pouring out their souls to God so affectionately for you, when their eye-strings and heart-strings were breaking. O put a value upon such mercies, for they are precious. It is a greater mercy to descend from praying parents than from the loins of nobles. See Job's pious practice (1. 5).

What a special mercy was it to us to have the excrescences of corruption nipped in the bud by their pious and careful discipline! We now understand what a critical and dangerous season youth is, the wonderful proclivity of that age to every thing that is evil. Why else are they called youthful lusts (2 Tim. 2. 22)? When David asks: 'Wherewithal shall a young man cleanse his way?' it is plainly enough implied in the very question that the way he takes lies through the pollutions of the world in his youth (Ps. 119. 9). When you find a David praying that God would 'not remember the sins of my youth'

(Ps. 25. 7), and a Job bitterly complaining that God 'made me to possess the iniquities of my youth' (13. 26), surely you cannot but reflect with a very thankful heart upon those happy means by which the corruption of your nature was happily prevented, or restrained in your youth.

And how great a mercy was it that we had parents who carefully instilled the good knowledge of God into our souls in our tender years? How diligent was Abraham in this duty (Gen. 18. 19), and David (1 Chron. 28. 9)! We have some of us had parents who might say to us, as the apostle: 'My little children of whom I travail in birth again until Christ be formed in you' (Gal. 4. 19). As they longed for us before they had us and rejoiced in us when they had us, so they could not endure to think that when they could have us no more, the devil should. As they thought no pains, care or cost too much for our bodies, to feed them, clothe and heal them; so did they think no prayers, counsels, or tears, too much for our souls, that they might be saved. They knew a parting time would come between them and us, and did strive to make it as easy and comfortable to them as they could, by leaving us in Christ and within the blessed bond of His covenant.

They were not glad that we had health and indifferent whether we had grace. They felt the miseries of our souls as much as of our bodies; and nothing was more desirable to them than that they might say in the great day: 'Lord, here am I and the children which thou hast given me.'

And was it not a special favour to us to have parents that went before us as patterns of holiness, and beat the path to heaven for us by their examples? They could say to us: 'those things ye have heard and seen in me, do' (Phil. 4. 9); and 'be ye followers of me, as also I am of Christ' (1 Cor. 11. 1). The parents' life is the child's copy. O, it is no common mercy to have a fair copy set before us, especially in the moulding age; we saw what they did, as well as heard what they said. It was Abraham's commendation, 'that he commanded his children, and his household after him, to keep the way of the Lord.' And such mercies some of us have had also.

Ah, my friends, let me beg you that you will take special notice of this Providence which so graciously wrought for you; and that your hearts may be more thoroughly warmed in the sense of it, compare your condition with others, and seriously consider the following.

How many children there are among us that are drawn headlong to hell by their cruel and ungodly parents, who teach them to curse and swear as soon as they can speak! Many families there are in which little other language is heard but what is the dialect of hell. These, like the old logs and small spray, are preparing for the fire of hell, where they must burn together. Of such children that Scripture will one day be verified, except they repent: 'He shall go to the generation of his fathers; they shall never see light' (Ps. 49. 19).

And how many families there are, though not so profane, who yet breed up their children vainly and sensually, and take no care what becomes of their souls, if they can but provide for their bodies (Job 21. 11)! If they can but teach them to carry their bodies, no matter if the devil actuate their souls. If they can but leave them lands or monies, they think they have very fully discharged their duties. O, what will the language be with which such parents and children shall greet each other at the judgment-seat, and in hell for ever!

And how many there are who are more sober and yet hate the least appearances of godliness in their children! Instead of cherishing, they do all that they can to break bruised reeds and quench smoking flax, to stifle and strangle the first appearances and offers they make towards Christ! They would rather accompany them to their graves than to Christ, doing all that in them lies, Herod-like, to kill Christ in the cradle! Ah, sirs, you little know what a mercy you enjoy or have enjoyed in godly parents and what a good lot Providence cast for you in this affair of your bodies and souls.

If any shall say this was not their case, they had little help heavenward from their parents, to such I reply as follows.

If you had little furtherance, yet own it as a special providence that you had no hindrance; or, if you had opposition, yet admire the grace of God in plucking you out by a wonderful distinguishing hand of mercy from among them and keeping alive the languishing sparks of grace amidst the floods of opposition. And learn from hence, if God give you a posterity of your own, to be so much the more strict and careful of family duties, by how much you have acutely felt the want of it in yourselves.

But seeing such a train of blessings, both as to this life and that to come, follow upon an holy education of children, I will not dismiss the point till I have discharged my duty in exhorting parents and children to their duties.

And first for you that are parents, or to whom the education of children is committed, I beseech you mind the duty which lies on you. That I may effectually press it, consider how near the relation is between you and your children, and therefore how much you are concerned in their happiness or misery. Consider but the Scripture account of the dearness of such relations, expressed by longings for them (Gen. 15. 2; 30. 1, 2), by our joy when we have them, as Christ expresses it (John 16. 21), the high value set on them (Gen. 42. 38), the sympathy with them in all their troubles (Mark 9. 22) and by our sorrow at parting (Gen. 37. 35). Now shall all this be to no purpose? For to what purpose do we desire them before we have them, rejoice in them when we have them, value them so highly, sympathize with them so tenderly, grieve for their death so excessively, if in the meantime no care be taken what shall become of them to eternity?

Consider how God has charged you with their souls, as well as bodies, and this appears by precepts directly laid upon you (Deut. 6. 6, 7; Eph. 6. 4) and by precepts laid on them to obey you (Eph. 6. 1), which plainly implies your duty as well as expresses theirs.

What shall comfort you at the parting time, if they die through your neglect in a Christless condition? O this is the cutting consideration: My child is in hell, and I did nothing to prevent it! I helped him there. Duty discharged is the only root of comfort in that day.

If you neglect to instruct them in the way of holiness, will the devil neglect to instruct them in the way of wickedness? No, no, if you will not teach them to pray, he will teach them to curse, swear and lie. If ground be uncultivated, weeds will spring up.

If the season of their youth is neglected, how little probability is there of any good fruit afterwards? Youth is the moulding age (Prov. 22. 6). How few are converted in old age? A twig is brought to any form, but grown limbs will not bend.

You are instrumental causes of all their spiritual misery, and that by generation and imitation. They lie spiritually dead of the plague which you brought home among them: 'Behold, I was shapen in iniquity, and in sin did my mother conceive [or warm] me' (Ps. 51. 5).

There is none in the world so likely as you to be instruments of their eternal good. You have peculiar advantages that no one else has; such as the interest you have in their affections; your opportunities to instil the knowledge of Christ into them, being daily with them (Deut. 6. 7); your knowledge of their character. If therefore you neglect, who shall help them?

Again, the consideration of the great day should move your bowels of pity for them. O remember that text: 'And I saw the dead small and great stand before God' (Rev. 20. 12). What a sad thing will it be, to see your dear children at Christ's left hand? O friends, do your utmost to prevent this misery. 'Knowing the terror of the Lord, we persuade men.'

And you, children, especially you that sprang from religious parents, I beseech you, obey their counsels, and tread in the steps of their pious examples. To press this, I offer the following considerations:

Your disobedience to them is a resisting of God's authority: 'Children, obey your parents in the Lord' (Eph. 6. 1). There is the command; your rebellion therefore runs higher than you think. It is not man, but God that you disobey; and for your disobedience God will punish you. It may be their tenderness will not suffer them, or you are grown beyond their correction.

All they can do is to complain to God, and if so, He will handle you more severely than they could do.

Your sin is greater than the sin of young heathens and in-fidels; and so will your account be also. O better, if a wicked child, that you had been the offspring of savage Indians, nay, of beasts, than of such parents. So many counsels disobeyed, hopes and prayers frustrated, will turn to sad aggravations.

It is usual with God to retaliate men's disobedience to their parents in kind; commonly our own children shall pay us home for it. I have read in a grave author of a wicked wretch that dragged his father along the house. The father begged him not to drag him beyond such a place, for, said he, I dragged my father no further. Oh, the sad, but just retributions of God!

And for you in whose hearts grace has been planted by the blessing of education, I beseech you to admire God's goodness to you in this providence. O what a happy lot has God cast for you! How few children are partakers of your mercies!

See that you honour such parents; the tie is double upon you so to do. Be you the joy of their hearts, and comfort of their lives, if they are alive. If not, yet still remember the mercy while you live, and tread in their pious path, that you and they may both rejoice together in the great day, and bless God for each other to all eternity.

3

THE WORK OF CONVERSION

═══

In nothing does Providence shine forth more gloriously in this world than in ordering the occasions, instruments and means of conversion of the people of God. However skilfully its hand had moulded your bodies, however tenderly it had preserved them and however bountifully it had provided for them; if it had not also ordered some means or other for your conversion, all the former favours and benefits it had done for you had meant little. This, O this, is the most excellent benefit you ever received from its hand. You are more indebted to it for this, than for all your other mercies. And in explaining this performance of Providence, I cannot but think your hearts must be deeply affected. This is a subject which every gracious heart loves to steep its thoughts in. It is certainly the sweetest history that ever they repeated; they love to think and talk of it. The places where, and instruments by whom this work was wrought are exceedingly endeared to them for the work's sake, yea, endeared to that degree, that, for many years after, their hearts have melted when they have but passed occasionally by those places or but seen the faces of those persons that were used as instruments in the hand of Providence for their good. As no doubt but Jacob's Bethel was ever after that night sweet to his thoughts (Gen. 48. 3), so other saints have had their Bethels as well as he. O blessed places, times, and instruments! O the deep, the sweet impressions, never to be erased out of the memory or heart, that this Providence has made upon those on whom it wrought this blessed effect at years of discretion, and in a more perceptible way!

But lest any poor soul should be discouraged by the display of this Providence because he cannot remember the time, place, instruments and manner when and by which conversion work was wrought, I will therefore premise this necessary distinction, to prevent injury to some, while I design benefit to others.

Conversion, as to the subjects of it, may be considered two ways; either as it is more clearly wrought in persons of riper years, who in their youthful days were more profane and vile; or upon persons in their tender years, into whose hearts grace was more imperceptibly and indiscernibly instilled by God's blessing upon pious education. In the former sort, the distinct acts of the Spirit, illuminating, convincing, humbling, drawing them to Christ and sealing them are more evident and discernible. In the latter, these are more obscure and confused. They can remember that God gave them an esteem and liking of godly persons, care of duty and conscience of sin; but as to the time, place, instruments and manner of the work, they can give but a slender account of them. However, if the work is savingly wrought in them, there is no reason they should be troubled because the circumstances of it are not so evident to them as they are to others. Let the substance and reality of the work appear and there is no reason to afflict yourselves because of the lack of evidence of such circumstances.

But where the circumstances as well as substance are clear to a man, when we can call to remembrance the time when, the place where, the instrument by whom that work was wrought, it must needs be exceedingly sweet, and they cannot but yield a fresh delight to the soul every time they are reflected upon.

There are many of the following occasions which, it may be, we took for stragglers when they first befell us, but they proved scouts sent out from the main body of Providence, which they make way for.

Now there are various things in those providences that respect this work, which are exceedingly sweet and taking, as namely :

The wonderful strangeness and unaccountableness of this work of Providence in casting us into the way and ordering the occasions, yea, the minutest circumstances about this work. Thus you find that the Eunuch, at that very instant when he was reading the prophet Esaias, had an interpreter, one among a thousand, that joins his chariot just as his mind was by a fit occasion prepared to receive the first light of the knowledge of Christ (Acts 8. 26–30).

And how strange was that change, however far it went, upon Naaman the Syrian (2 Kings 5. 1–4)! that the Syrians in their incursion should bring away this girl – likely her beauty was the inducement – and she must be presented to Naaman's wife, and relate to her the power of God that accompanied the prophet; though you find in that particular case there had never been an instance given before (Luke 4. 27). Doubtless the whole of this affair was guided by the signal direction of Providence.

So for the conversion of the Samaritans, it is observed that Christ must needs go that way (John 4. 4) – it lay just in the road between Judea and Galilee – and at the sixth hour, i.e., high noon, he rests himself upon Jacob's well, still seeming to have no other design but his own refreshment by sitting and drinking there. But O what a train of blessed providences follow this which seemed but an accidental thing! First the woman of Samaria and then many more in that city are brought to believe in Christ (verses 29 and 41).

It is noted by Melchior Adams in the Life of Junius how much of an atheist he was in his younger years; but in order to bring about his conversion to God, first, a wonderful preservation of his life in a public tumult at Lyons in France must take place, which forces from him the acknowledgment of a Deity. Then his father sends for him home and with much gentleness persuades him to read the Scriptures. He lights upon the first of John, and with it he feels a divine supernatural majesty and power seizing his soul, which brought him over by a complete conversion to Jesus Christ. Thus, as the woman of Tekoa told David, does God devise means to bring back His banished (2 Sam. 14. 14).

Lavater tells us that many Spanish soldiers, going into the wars of Germany, were there converted to Christ, by going into the cities and towns where godly ministers and Christians were.

Robert Bolton, though an excellent scholar, yet in his younger years he was a very irreligious person and a jeerer of holy men; but being cast into the company of godly Mr Peacock was by him brought to repentance and proved a famous instrument in the Church of Christ.

A scrap of paper, accidentally coming to view, has been used as an occasion of conversion. This was the case of a minister in Wales, who had two livings, but took little care of either. Being at a fair, he bought something at a pedlar's stall, and tore off a leaf of Mr Perkins' Catechism to wrap it in, and reading a line or two in it, God sent it home so as it did the work.

The marriage of a godly man into a carnal family has been ordered by Providence for the conversion and salvation of many therein. Thus we read in the life of that renowned English worthy, John Bruen, that in his second match it was agreed that he should have one year's diet in his mother-in-law's house. During his abode there that year the Lord was pleased by this means graciously to work upon her soul, as also upon his wife's sister and half-sister, their brothers William and Thomas Fox, with one or two of the servants in that family.

The reading of a good book has been the means of bringing others to Christ. And thus we find many of the German divines converted by reading Luther's books; yea, and what is more strange, Sleyden, in his Commentary, tells us that Vergerius, though he were an eye and ear witness to that doleful case of Spira, which one would think should move a stone, yet still continued so firm to the pope's interest that when he fell into some suspicion among the cardinals he resolved to purge himself by writing a book against the German apostates. But while he read the Protestant books, out of no other design but to confute them, while he is weighing the arguments, he is himself convinced and brought to Christ. He, finding himself thus overcome by the truth, imparts his conviction to his brother, also a zealous papist. This brother deplores the misery of his case and seeks to reclaim him; but Vergerius entreating him to weigh well the Protestant arguments, he also yields, and so both immediately gave themselves to preaching justification by the free grace of God through the blood of Christ.

Yea, not only the reading of a book or hearing a minister, but, which is most remarkable, the very mistake or forgetfulness of a minister has been improved by Providence for this end and purpose. Augustine, once preaching to his congregation, forgot the argument which first he proposed and attacked the error of the Manichees beside his first intention. By this discourse he converted one Firmus, his hearer, who fell down at his feet weeping and confessing he had lived a Manichee many years.

Another I knew who, going to preach, took up another Bible than that he designed, in which, not only missing his notes but the chapter also in which his text lay, was put to some loss thereby. But after a short pause he resolved to speak on any other Scripture that might be presented to him and accordingly read that text: 'The Lord is not slack concerning his promise, as some men count slackness' (2 Pet. 3. 9). And though he had nothing prepared, yet the Lord helped him to speak both methodically and pertinently from it, by which discourse a gracious change was wrought upon one in the congregation who has since given good evidence of a sound conversion and acknowledged this sermon to be the first and only means thereof.

The accompanying of others in a neighbourly civil visit has been overruled to the same end. Thus many of the Jews accompanied Mary unto Bethany, designing only to manifest their civil respect, but there they met Christ, saw the things which He did, and believed on Him (John 11. 45).

Firmin * tells us of one who had lived many years in a town where Christ had been as clearly and as long preached as in any town in England. This man, when he was about seventy-six years of age, went to visit a sick neighbour. 'A Christian friend of mine,' says my author, 'came to see him also, and finding this old man there, whom he judged to be one that lived upon his own stock, civility, good works, etc., he purposely fell into that discourse, to shew how many persons lived upon their duties, but never came to Christ. The old man sitting by the bedside heard him, and God was pleased to convince him that he was such a person, who had lived upon himself without Christ to that day; and would say afterwards, Had I died before three-score and sixteen, I had perished, for I knew not Christ.'

The committing of a godly man to prison has been the method of Providence to save the soul of a poor keeper. So Paul was made a prisoner to make his keeper a spiritual freeman (Acts 16. 27). The like success had Dr Barnes in Queen Mary's days, who afterwards celebrated the Lord's Supper in prison with his converted keeper.

The scattering of ministers and Christians by persecution from cities and towns into the ignorant and barbarous parts of the country, has been the way of Providence to find out and bring home some lost sheep that were found there to Jesus Christ (Acts 8. 1, 4). The like signal event has since followed upon the like scattering of godly ministers, of which there are many outstanding instances at this day.

A servant running away from his master, probably out of no other design but to live an idle life, yet falling into such places and companies as Providence ordered in a design to him unknown, has thereby been brought to be the servant of Christ. This was the very case of Onesimus who ran away from his master Philemon to Rome, where by a strange Providence, possibly a mere curiosity to see the prisoners, he there

* Giles Firmin (1614–97), Puritan minister of Shalford, Essex and author of *The Real Christian*.

falls into Paul's hands, who begat him to Christ in his bonds (Philemon 10-16).

Going to hear a sermon in jest has proved some men's conversion in earnest. The above-named Mr Firmin tells us of a notorious drunkard whom the drunkards called 'father' that one day would needs go to hear what Wilson said, out of no other design, it seems, but to scoff at that holy man. But in the prayer before the sermon his heart began to thaw, and when he read his text: 'Sin no more, lest a worse thing come unto thee' (John 5. 14), he could not contain, and in that sermon the Lord changed his heart, though so bitter an enemy that the minister on lecture-days was afraid to go to church before his shop door. 'Lo, these are parts of his ways, but how small a portion is known of him?'

The dropping of some grave and weighty word accidentally in the presence of vain carnal persons, the death of a husband, wife or child, a fit of sickness, with a thousand other such like occasions, have been thus improved by Providence to the conversion of souls.

And no less remarkable and wonderful are the designs of Providence in ordering the removals and governing the movements of ministers from place to place, for the conversion of souls. Thus often it carries them to places where they did not intend to go, God having, unknown to them, some elect vessels there who must be called by the Gospel.

Thus Paul and Timothy, a sweet and lovely pair, when they were travelling through Phrygia and Galatia, were forbidden to preach the Word in Asia, to which probably their minds inclined (Acts 16. 6), and when 'they essayed to go into Bithynia, the Spirit suffered them not' (verse 7). But a man of Macedonia, i.e., an angel in the shape or habit of a man of that country, appeared to Paul in a vision and prayed him saying: 'Come over into Macedonia, and help us' (verse 9), and there did God open the heart of Lydia.

I knew a pious minister, now with God, who, falling in his study upon a very rousing subject, intended for his own congregation, was strongly moved, when he had finished it, to go to a rude, vile, profane people about five miles off and first preach it to them. After many wrestlings with himself, not being willing to quench any motion that might be supposed to come from the Spirit of God, he obeyed and went to this people, who had then no minister of their own and few durst come among them. And there did the Lord, beyond all expectation, open a door, and several profane ones received Christ in that place and engaged this minister to a weekly lecture among them, in which many souls were won to God.

The same holy man at another time, being upon a journey, passed by a company of vain persons, who were wrestling upon a green near the road. Just as he came near the place one of them had thrown his antagonist and stood triumphing in his strength and activity. This good man rode up to them, and turning his speech to this person, told him : 'Friend, I see that you are a strong man, but let not the strong man glory in his strength : you must know that you are not to wrestle with flesh and blood, but with principalities and powers, and spiritual wickednesses. How sad will it be that Satan should at last trip up the heels of your hope, and give you an eternal overthrow!' After about a quarter of an hour's serious discourse upon this subject, he left them and went on his journey, but this discourse made such an impression, that the person had no rest till he confided his trouble to a godly minister, who wisely following the work upon his soul, saw at last the blessed issue thereof in the gracious change of the person, of which he afterwards gave the minister a joyful account. O how unsearchable are the methods of Providence in this matter!

Nay, what is yet more wonderful, the Providence of God has sometimes ordered the very malice of Satan and wickedness of men as an occasion of eternal good to their souls. A very memorable example of this I shall here give the reader, faithfully relating what, not many years past, occurred in my own observation in this place, to the astonishment of many spectators.

In the year 1673, there came into this port* a ship of Poole,

*Dartmouth

in her return from Virginia. In this ship was one of that place, a lusty young man of twenty-three years of age, who was surgeon in the ship. This person in the voyage fell into a deep melancholy, which the devil greatly improved to serve his own design for the ruin of this poor man. However, it pleased the Lord to restrain him from any attempts upon his own life until he arrived here. But shortly after his arrival, upon the Lord's day, early in the morning, being in bed with his brother, he took a knife prepared for that purpose and cut his own throat, and then leapt out of the bed, and though the wound was deep and large, yet thinking it might not soon enough dispatch his wretched life, desperately thrust it into his stomach and so lay wallowing in his own blood till his brother awakening made a cry for help. Hereupon a physician and a surgeon coming in, found the wound in his throat mortal, and all they could do at present was only to stitch it and apply a plaster with the design rather to enable him to speak for a little while than with any expectation of cure; for before that, he breathed through the wound and his voice was inarticulate.

In this condition I found him that morning, and apprehending him to be within a few minutes of eternity, I laboured to work upon his heart the sense of his condition, telling him I had but little time to do anything for him, and therefore I desired him to let me know what his own apprehensions of his present condition were. He told me he hoped in God for eternal life. I replied that I feared his hopes were ill-grounded, for the Scripture tells us: 'No murderer hath eternal life abiding in him.' But this was self-murder, the grossest of all murders, and insisting upon the aggravation and heinousness of the fact, I perceived his vain confidence began to fall and some meltings of heart appeared in him. He then began to lament with many tears his sin and misery and asked me if there might yet be hope for one that had destroyed himself and shed his own blood. I replied, the sin indeed is great but not unpardonable, and if the Lord gave him repentance unto life, and faith to apply to Jesus Christ, it should be certainly pardoned to him.

Finding him unacquainted with these things, I explained to him the nature and necessity of faith and repentance, which he greedily sucked in and with great vehemence cried to God that He would work them upon his soul, and intreated me also to pray with him and for him that it might be so. I prayed with him and the Lord thawed his heart exceedingly in that duty. Loth he was to part with me, but the duties of the day necessitating me to leave him, I briefly summed up what was most necessary in my parting counsel to him and took my leave, never expecting to see him more in this world. But beyond my own and all men's expectation, he continued all that day and panted most ardently after Jesus Christ. No discourses pleased him but Christ and faith, and in this frame I found him in the evening. He rejoiced greatly to see me again and intreated me to continue my discourses upon these subjects; and after all told me: 'Sir, the Lord has given me repentance for this sin; yea, and for every other sin. I see the evil of sin now, so as I never saw it before. O, I loathe myself; I am a vile creature in my own eyes! I do also believe; Lord, help my unbelief. I am heartily willing to take Christ upon His own terms. One thing only troubles me. I doubt this bloody sin will not be pardoned. Will Jesus Christ apply His blood to me, that have shed my own blood?' I told him Christ shed His blood even for them that with wicked hands had shed the blood of Christ, and that was a sin of deeper guilt than his. 'Well,' said he, 'I will cast myself upon Christ. Let him do by me what he will.' And so I parted with him that night.

Next morning the wounds were to be opened, and then the opinion of the surgeons was that he would immediately expire. Accordingly, at his desire, I came that morning and found him in a most serious frame. I prayed with him, and then the wound in his stomach was opened, and by this time the ventricle itself was swollen out of the orifice of the wound and lay like a livid discoloured tripe upon his body and was also cut through; so that all concluded it was impossible for him to live. However they stitched the wound in the stomach, enlarged the orifice and fomented it, and wrought it again into his body, and so stitching up the skin, left him to the disposal of Providence.

But so it was that both the deep wound in his throat and this in his stomach healed, and the more dangerous wound sin had made upon his soul, was, I trust, effectually healed also. I spent many hours with him in that sickness, and, after his return home, received this account from Mr Samuel Hardy, a minister in that town, part of which I shall transcribe.

Dear Sir,

I was much troubled at the sad providence in your town, but did much rejoice that he fell into such hands for his body and soul. You have taken much pains with him, and I hope to good purpose. I think, if ever a great and thorough work were done such a way, it is now, and if never the like, I am persuaded now it is. Never grow weary of such good works. One such instance is, methinks, enough to make you to abound in the work of the Lord all your days. . . .

O how unsearchable are the ways of Providence in leading men to Christ! Let none be encouraged by this to sin that grace may abound. These are rare and singular instances of the mercy of God, and such as no presumptuous sinner can expect to find. It is only recited here to the honour of Providence, which works for the recovery of sinners in ways that we do not understand.

As Providence orders very strange occasions to awaken and arouse souls at first, so it works no less wonderfully in carrying on the work to perfection. This it does in two ways.

First, by quickening and reviving dying convictions and troubles for sin. Souls, after their first awakening, are apt to lose the sense and impression of their first troubles for sin; but Providence is vigilant to prevent it, and effectually prevents it. Sometimes Providence directs the minister to some discourse or passage that shall fall as pat as if the case of such a person had been studied by him and designedly spoken to. How often have I found this in the cases of many souls who have professed they have stood amazed to hear the very thoughts of their hearts revealed by the preacher, who knew nothing of them! Sometimes Providence directs them to some proper rousing Scripture that suits their present case, and sometimes it permits them to fall into some new sin which awakens all their former troubles again and puts a new efficacy and activity into the conscience. The world is full of instances of all these cases, and because most Christians have experience of these things in themselves, it will be needless to recite them here. Search but a few years back, and you may remember that, according to this account, at least in some particulars, Providence ordered the matter with you. Have you not found some rod or other prepared by Providence to rouse you out of your security? Why, this is so common a thing with Christians that they many times presage an affliction coming from the frames they find their own hearts in.

Secondly, Providence gives great assistance to the work of the Spirit upon the soul, by ordering, supporting, relieving and cheering means, to prop up and comfort the soul when it is over-burdened and ready to sink in the depths of troubles. I remember Mr Bolton gives us one instance which fits both these cases, the reviving of convictions, and seasonable supports in the depths of troubles. It is of a person that by convictions had been fetched off from his wicked companions and entered into a reformed course of life. But after this, through the enticement of his old companions, the subtlety of Satan and corruption of his own heart, he again relapsed into the ways of sin. Then was providentially brought to his view that Scripture, Proverbs 1. 24–26. This renewed his trouble, yea, aggravated it to a greater height than ever, insomuch that he could scarcely think, as it seems by the relation, his sin could be pardoned. But in this condition that text, Luke 17. 4, was presented to him, which sweetly settled him in a sure and glorious peace.

Nor can we here forget that miraculous work of Providence, in a time of great extremity, which was wrought for that good gentlewoman Mrs Honeywood, who under a deep and sad desertion, refused and put off all comfort, seeming to despair utterly of the grace and mercy of God. A worthy minister being one day with her and reasoning against her desperate conclusions, she took a Venice-glass from the table and said: 'Sir, I am as sure to be damned as this glass is to be broken', and therewith threw it forcibly to the ground. But to the astonishment of both, the glass remained whole and sound, which the minister taking up with admiration, rebuked her presumption and showed her what a wonder Providence had wrought for her satisfaction, and it greatly altered the attitude of her mind. 'How unsearchable are his judgments, and his ways past finding out!' (Rom. 11. 33). 'Lo, these are parts of his ways, but how little a portion is heard of him!' (Job 26. 14).

And now let me expostulate a little with your soul, reader. Have you been duly aware of your obligation to Providence for this inestimable favour? O what it has done for you! There are various kinds of mercies conveyed to men by the hand of Providence, but none like this; in all the treasury of its benefits none is found like this. Did it cast you into the way of conversion, and order the means and occasions of it for you, when you little thought of any such thing? How dear and sweet should the remembrance of it be to your soul! methinks it should astonish and melt you every time you reflect upon it. Such mercies should never grow stale or look like common things to you, for do but seriously consider the following particulars.

How surprising was the mercy which Providence performed for you in that day! Providence had a design upon you for your eternal good, which you did not understand. The time of mercy was now fully come; the decree was now ready to bring forth that mercy, with which it had gone big from eternity, and its gracious design must be executed by the hand of Providence, so far as concerned the external means and instruments. How aptly did it cause all things to fall in with that design, though you did not know the meaning of it? Look over all the before-mentioned examples, and you will see the blessed work of conversion begun upon those souls, when they minded it no more than Saul did a kingdom that morning he went out 'to seek his father's asses' (1 Sam. 9. 3, 20). Providence might truly have said to you in that day, as Christ said to Peter: 'What I do thou knowest not now, but thou shalt know it hereafter' (John 13. 7). God's thoughts are not as our thoughts; but as the heavens are higher than the earth so are His thoughts higher than ours, and His ways than our ways. Little did Zacchæus think when he climbed up into the sycamore tree to see Christ as He passed that way what a design of mercy Christ had upon him, who took thence the occasion of becoming both his Guest and Saviour (Luke 19. 5–8). And as little did some of you think what the aim of Providence was when you went, some out of custom, others out of curiosity, if not worse motives, to hear such a sermon. O how stupendous are the ways of God!

What a distinguishing and seasonable mercy was ushered in by Providence in that day! It brought you to the means of salvation in a good hour. In the very nick of time, when the angel troubled the waters, you were brought to the pool (John 5. 4). Now the accepted day was come, the Spirit was in the ordinance or providence that converted you, and you were set in the way of it. It may be you had heard many hundred sermons before, but nothing would stick till now, because the hour was not come. The Lord did, as it were, call in the word for such a man, such a woman, and Providence said: 'Lord, here he is, I have brought him before thee.' There were many others under that sermon that received no such mercy. You yourselves had heard many before, but not to that advantage, as it is said: 'And many lepers were in Israel in the time of Eliseus the prophet; and none of them was cleansed, saving Naaman the Syrian' (Luke 4. 27). So there were many poor, unconverted souls beside you under the Word that day, and it may be, to none of them was salvation sent that day but to you. O blessed Providence that set you in the way of mercy at that time!

What a weighty and important mercy was providentially directed to your souls that day. There are mercies of all sizes and kinds in the hands of Providence to dispense to the sons of men. Its left hand is full of blessings as well as its right. It has health and riches, honours and pleasures, as well as Christ and salvation to dispense. The world is full of its left hand favours, but the blessings of its right hand are invaluably precious and few there be that receive them. It performs thousands of kind offices for men; but among them all, this is the chiefest, to lead and direct them to Christ. For consider, of all mercies, this comes through most and greatest difficulties (Eph. 1. 19, 20).

This is a spiritual mercy, excelling in dignity of nature all others, more than gold excels the dirt under your feet (Rev. 3. 18). One such gift is worth thousands of other mercies.

This is a mercy immediately flowing out of the fountain of God's electing love, a mercy never dropped into any but an elect vessel (1 Thess. 1. 4, 5).

This is a mercy that infallibly secures salvation; for as we may argue from conversion to election, looking back, so from conversion to salvation, looking forward (Heb. 6. 9).

Lastly, this is an eternal mercy, one which will stick by you when father, mother, wife, children, estate, honours, health and life shall fail you (John 4. 14).

O, therefore, set a special mark upon that Providence that set you in the way of this mercy. It has performed that for you which all the ministers on earth and angels in heaven could never have performed. This is a mercy that puts weight and value into the smallest circumstance that relates to it.

4

OUR EMPLOYMENT

Another excellent performance of Providence, respecting the good of both your bodies and souls, concerns that employment and calling it has ordered for you in this world. It has not only an eye upon your well-being in the world to come, but upon your well-being in this world also, and that very much depends upon the station and vocation to which it calls you.

Now the Providence of God with respect to our civil callings may be displayed very takingly in the following particulars.

In directing you to a calling in your youth, and not permitting you to live an idle, useless and sinful life, as many do who are but burdens to the earth, the wens of the body politic, serving only to disfigure and drain it, to eat what others earn. Sin brought in sweat (Gen. 3. 19), but now, not to sweat increases sin. He that lives idly cannot live honestly, as is plainly enough intimated (1 Thess. 4. 11, 12). But when God puts men into a lawful calling, in which the labour of their hands or heads is sufficient for them, it is a very valuable mercy; for in so doing they 'eat their own bread' (2 Thess. 3. 12). Many a sad temptation is happily prevented, and they are ordinarily furnished by it for works of mercy to others, and surely 'it is more blessed to give than to receive.'

In ordering you to such callings and employments in the world as are not only lawful in themselves but most suitable to you. There are many persons employed in sinful trades and arts, merely to furnish other men's lusts. They do not only sin in their employments, but their very employments are sinful. They trade for hell, and are factors for the devil. Demetrius and the craftsmen at Ephesus got their estates by making shrines for Diana (Acts 19. 24, 25), i.e., little cases or boxes with folding leaves, within which the image of that idol sat enshrined. These were carried about by the people in procession in honour of their idol. And at this day, how many wicked arts and employments are there invented, and multitudes of persons maintained by them, merely to gratify the pride and wantonness of a debauched age!

Now to have an honest and lawful employment, in which you do not dishonour God in benefiting yourselves, is no small mercy. But if it is not only lawful in itself, but suited to your genius and strength, there is a double mercy in it. Some poor creatures are engaged in callings that eat up their time and strength, and make their lives very uncomfortable to them. They have not only consuming and wasting employments in the world, but such as allow them little or no time for their general calling, and yet all this does but keep them and theirs alive. Therefore, if God has fitted you with an honest employment in which you have less toil than others, and more time for heavenly exercises, ascribe this benefit to the special care of Providence for you.

In settling you in such an employment and calling in the world, as possibly neither yourselves nor parents could ever expect you should attain to. There are among us such persons as, on this account, are signally obliged to divine Providence. God has put them into such a way as neither they nor their parents ever planned. For look how the needle in the compass turns now this way, then that way, and never ceases moving till it settles to the north point; just so it is in our settlement in the world. A child is now designed for this, then for that, but at last settles in that way of employment to which Providence designed him. How strangely are things wheeled about by Providence! Not what we or our parents, but what God designed shall take place. Amos was very meanly employed at first, but God designed him for a more honourable and comfortable calling (Amos 7. 14, 15). David followed the ewes, and probably never raised his thoughts to higher things in the days of his youth; but God made him the royal shepherd of a better flock (Ps. 78. 70, 71). Peter and Andrew were employed as fishermen, but Christ calls them from that to a higher calling, to be 'fishers of men' (Matt. 4. 18, 19). Pareus, when he was fourteen years old, was by the instigation of his stepmother placed with an apothecary; but Providence so wrought that he was taken off from that and fitted for the ministry, in which he became a fruitful and eminent instrument to the Church. James Andreas was, by reason of his father's inability to keep him at school, designed for a carpenter, but was afterwards, by the persuasion of friends and assistance of the church-flock, sent to Stuttgart, and thence to the University, and so attained to a very eminent station of service to the Church. A master builder, Œcolampadius, was by his father designed for a merchant; but his mother, by urgent entreaties, prevailed to keep him at school, and this man was a blessed instrument in the reformation of religion. I might easily cite multitudes of such instances, but a taste may suffice.

In securing your estates from ruin. 'Hast thou not made an hedge about him, and all that he hath?' (Job 1. 10). This is the enclosure of Providence, which secures to us what by its favour we acquire in the way of honest industry.

In making your calling sufficient for you. It was the prayer of Moses for the tribe of Judah: 'Let his hands be sufficient for him' (Deut. 33. 7), and it is no small mercy if yours be so to you. Some there are that have work, but not strength to go through with it; others have strength, but no employment for it. Some have hands, and work for them; but it is not sufficient for them and theirs. If God bless your labours, so as to give you and yours necessary supports and comfort in the world by it, it is a choice providence, and with all thankfulness to be acknowledged.

If any that fear God shall complain that, although they have a calling, yet it is a hard and laborious one, which takes up too much of their time which they would gladly employ in other and better work, I answer that it is likely that the wisdom of Providence foresaw this to be the most suitable and proper employment for you; and if you had more ease and rest, you might have more temptations than now you have. The strength and time which is now taken up in your daily labours, in which you serve God, might otherwise have been spent upon such lusts in which you might have served the devil.

Moreover, hereby it may be your health is the better preserved, and natural refreshments made the sweeter to you. 'The sleep of a labouring man is sweet, whether he eat little or much : but the abundance of the rich will not suffer him to sleep' (Eccl. 5. 12).

And as to the service of God, if your hearts are spiritual, you may enjoy much communion with God in your very employments, and you have some intervals and respites for that purpose. Have you not more spare hours than you employ to that end?

'But all my labours will scarcely suffice to procure me and mine the necessaries of life. I am kept short and low to what others are, and this is a sad affliction.'

Though the wisdom of Providence has ordered you a lower and poorer condition than others, yet consider how many there are that are lower than you in the world. You have but little of the world, yet others have less. Read the description of those persons (Job 30. 4, etc.). If God has given you but a small portion of the world, yet if you are godly He has promised never to forsake you (Heb. 13. 5). Providence has ordered that condition for you which is really best for your eternal good. If you had more of the world than you have, your heads and hearts might not be able to manage it to your advantage. A small boat must have but a narrow sail. You have not lacked hitherto the necessities of life, and are commanded 'having food and raiment (though none of the finest) to be therewith content.' 'A little that a righteous man hath is better than the riches of many wicked' (Ps. 37. 16): better in the acquisition, sweeter in the fruition, and more comfortable in the account.

Well then, if Providence has so disposed of you all, that you can eat your own bread, and so advantageously directed some of you to employments that afford, not only necessities for yourselves and families, but a surplus for works of mercy to others, and all this brought about for you in a way you did not plan; let God be owned and honoured in this providence. Will you not henceforth call Him : 'My Father, the guide of my youth' (Jer. 3. 4)? Surely it was the Lord that guided you to settle as you did in those days of your youth; you reap at this day, and may to your last day, the fruits of those early providences in your youth.

Now see that you walk answerably to the obligations of Providence in this particular; and see to it in the fear of God that you do not abuse any of those things to His dishonour which He has wrought for your comfort. To prevent this, I will here drop a few needful cautions, and conclude this particular point.

Do not be slothful and idle in your vocations. It is said that Augustus built an Apragapolis, a city void of business; but I am sure God never erected any city, town or family to that end. The command to Adam (Gen. 3. 19) no doubt reaches all his posterity, and Gospel-commands bind it upon Christians (Rom. 12. 11; 1 Thess. 4. 11). If you are negligent, you cannot be innocent.

And yet do not be so intent upon your particular callings as to make them interfere with your general calling. Beware you do not lose your God in the crowd and hurry of earthly business. Mind that solemn warning : 'But they that will be rich fall into temptation and a snare, and into many foolish and hurtful lusts, which drown men in destruction and perdition' (1 Tim. 6. 9). The inhabitants of Oenoe, a dry island near Athens, bestowed much labour to draw in a river to water it and make it fruitful. But when the sluices were opened, the waters flowed so abundantly that it overflowed the island and drowned the inhabitants. The application is obvious. It was an excellent saying of Seneca : 'I do not give, but lend myself to business.'

Remember always the success of your callings and earthly

employments is by divine blessing, not human diligence alone. 'But thou shalt remember the Lord thy God; for it is he that giveth thee power to get wealth' (Deut. 8. 18). The devil himself was so far orthodox as to acknowledge it : 'Hast not thou made an hedge about him, and about his house, and about all that he hath on every side? Thou hast blessed the work of his hands' (Job 1. 10). Recommend therefore your affairs to God in prayer. 'Delight thyself also in the Lord; and he shall give thee the desires of thine heart. Commit thy way unto the Lord; trust also in him, and he shall bring it to pass' (Ps. 37. 4, 5). And do not meddle with that which you cannot recommend to God in prayer for a blessing.

Be well satisfied in that station and employment in which Providence has placed you, and do not so much as wish yourself in another. 'Let every man abide in the same calling wherein he was called' (1 Cor. 7. 20). Providence is wiser than you, and you may be confident it has suited all things better to your eternal good than you could do had you been left to your own option.

5

FAMILY AFFAIRS

═══════

That Providence has a special hand in our marriage is evident both from Scripture assertions and the acknowledgments of holy men, who in that great event of their lives have still owned and acknowledged the directing hand of Providence. Take an instance of both. The Scripture plainly asserts the dominion of Providence over this affair: 'A prudent wife is from the Lord' (Prov. 19. 14). 'Whoso findeth a wife findeth a good thing, and obtaineth favour of the Lord' (Prov. 18. 22). So for children: 'Lo, children are an heritage of the Lord; and the fruit of the womb is his reward' (Ps. 127. 3).

And it has ever been the practice of holy men to seek the Lord for direction and counsel, when they have been changing their condition. No doubt but Abraham's encouragement in that case was the fruit of prayer. His pious servant also, who was employed in that affair, did both earnestly seek counsel of God, and thankfully acknowledge His gracious providence in guiding it (Gen. 24. 7, 12, 26, 27).

The same we may observe in children, the fruit of marriage (1 Sam. 1. 20; Luke 1. 13, 14). Now the Providence of God may be in various ways displayed for the engaging of our hearts in love to the God of our mercies.

There is very much of Providence seen *in appointing the parties for each other*. In this the Lord often goes beyond our thoughts and plans; yea, and often crosses men's desires and designs to their great advantage. Not what they expect, but what His infinite wisdom judges best and most beneficial for them takes place. Hence it is that probabilities are so often dashed, and things remote and utterly improbable are brought about, in very strange and unaccountable methods of Providence.

There is much of Providence seen *in the harmony and agreeableness of temperaments and dispositions*, from which a very great part of the tranquillity and comforts of our lives results. Or at least, though natural temperament and education did not so much harmonize before, yet they do so after they come under the ordinance of God : 'And they shall be one flesh' (Gen. 2. 24). Not one only in respect of God's institution, but one in respect of love and affection, that those who so lately were mere strangers to each other are now endeared to a degree beyond the nearest relations in blood : 'Therefore shall a man leave father and mother, and shall cleave to his wife, and they shall be one flesh.'

But Providence is especially remarkable *in making one instrumental to the eternal good of the other* : 'What knowest thou, O wife, whether thou shalt save thy husband? or how knowest thou, O man, whether thou shalt save thy wife?' (1 Cor. 7. 16). Hence is that grave exhortation to the wives of unbelieving husbands to win them by their conversation, which should be to them instead of an ordinance (1 Pet. 3. 1).

Or if both are gracious, then what singular assistance and mutual help is hereby gained to the furtherance of their eternal good whilst they live together 'as heirs together of the grace of life' (1 Pet. 3. 7). O blessed Providence that directed such into so intimate relation on earth, who shall inherit together the common salvation of heaven!

How much of Providence is seen *in children, the fruit of marriage*! To have any posterity in the earth, and not be left altogether as a dry tree; to have comfort and joy in them is a special providence, importing a special mercy to us. To have the breaches made upon our families repaired, is a providence to be owned with a thankful heart. When God shall say to a man, as he speaks in another case to the Church : 'The children which thou shalt have after thou hast lost the other, shall say again in thine ears: The place is too strait for me' (Isa 49. 20).

And these providences will appear more affectingly sweet and lovely to you, if you but compare God's allotments to you with what He has allotted to many others in the world. For do but look around and you will find multitudes unequally yoked, to the embittering of their lives, whose relations are clogs and hindrances both in things temporal and spiritual. Yea, we find an account in Scripture of gracious persons, a great part of whose comfort in this world has been split upon this rock. Abigail was a discreet and virtuous woman, but very unsuitably matched to a churlish Nabal (1 Sam. 25. 25). What a temptation to the neglect of a known duty prevailed upon the renowned Moses by the means of Zipporah his wife (Exod. 4. 24, 25). David had his scoffing Michal (2 Sam. 6. 20), and patient Job no small addition to all his other afflictions from the wife of his bosom, who should have been a support to him in the day of his troubles (Job 19. 17).

No doubt but God sanctifies such rods to His people's good. If Socrates knew how to improve his affliction in his Xanthippe to the increase of his patience, much more will they who converse with God under all providences, whether sweet or bitter. Nevertheless this must be acknowledged to be a sad stroke upon any person, and such as maims them upon the working hand, by unfitting them for duty (1 Pet. 3. 7) and cuts off much of the comfort of life also.

How many there are who never enjoy the comfortable fruits of marriage, but are denied the sight, or at least the enjoyment of children! 'Thus saith the Lord: Write this man childless' (Jer. 22. 30), or if they have children, yet cannot enjoy them: 'Though they bring up their children, yet will I bereave them that there shall not be a man left' (Hosea 9. 12), who only bear for the grave, and have their expectations raised for a greater affliction to themselves.

And it is no rare or unusual thing to see children and near relations the greatest instruments of affliction to their parents and friends, so that after all their other sorrows and troubles in the world, nearest relations bring up the rear of sorrows and prove greater griefs than any other. O how many parents have complained with the tree in the fable, that their very hearts have been riven asunder with those wedges that were cut out of their own bodies! What a grief was Esau to Isaac and Rebecca (Gen. 26. 34, 35)! what scourges were Absalom and Amnon to David!

Well then, if God has set 'the solitary in families' (Ps. 68. 6), built a house for the desolate, given you comfortable relations, which are springs of daily comfort and refreshment to you, you are upon many accounts engaged to walk answerably to these gracious providences. And that you may understand wherein that decorum and agreeable comportment with these providences consists, take up the sense of your duty in these brief hints:

Ascribe to God the glory of all those providential works which yield you comfort. You see a wise, directing, governing Providence, which has disposed and ordered all things beyond your own plans and designs: 'The way of man is not in himself; it is not in man that walketh to direct his steps' (Jer. 10. 23). Not what you planned, but what a higher counsel than yours determined is come to pass. Good Jacob, when God had made him the father of a family, admired God in the mercy. 'For with my staff,' said he, 'I passed over this Jordan, and now I am become two bands' (Gen. 32. 10). And how this mercy humbles and melts him! 'I am not worthy of the least of all the mercies, and of all the truth which thou hast showed unto thy servant.'

Be exact in discharging the duties of those relations which so gracious a Providence has led you into. Do not abuse the effects of so much mercy and love to you. The Lord expects praise wherever you have comfort. This aggravated David's sin, that he should dare to abuse so great love and mercy as God had shown him in his family relations (2 Sam. 12. 7–9).

Use relations to the end Providence designed them. Walk together as co-heirs of the grace of life; study to be mutual blessings to each other; so walk in your relations that the

[84]

parting day may be sweet. Death will shortly break up the family; and then nothing but the sense of duty discharged, or the neglects pardoned, will give comfort.

Another gracious performance of Providence for us is seen in making provision from time to time for us and our families. I the rather put these providences together in this place because I find the Scripture does so. 'Yet setteth he the poor on high from affliction, and maketh him families like a flock' (Ps. 107. 41).

You know the promises God has made to His people: 'The young lions do lack and suffer hunger, but they that seek the Lord shall not want any good thing' (Ps. 34. 10). And have you not also seen the constant performance of it? Cannot you give the same answer, if the same question were propounded to you, which the disciples did: 'When I sent you without purse, and scrip, and shoes, lacked ye anything? and they said, Nothing' (Luke 22. 35)? Can you not with Jacob call him 'the God which fed me all my life long'? (Gen. 48. 15). Surely 'he hath given meat unto them that fear him; he will ever be mindful of his covenant' (Ps. 111. 5).

To display this Providence we will consider it in the following particulars:

The assiduity and constancy of the care of Providence for the saints. His mercies 'are new every morning' (Lam. 3. 23). It is not just the supply of one or two pressing needs, but all your wants, as they grow from day to day through all your days. 'The God which fed me all my life long' (Gen. 48. 15). The care of Providence runs parallel with the line of life: 'Hearken unto me, O house of Jacob, and all the remnant of the house of Israel, which are borne by me from the belly, which are carried from the womb: and even to your old age I am he, and even to hoar hairs will I carry you: I have made, and I will bear, even I will carry, and will deliver you' (Isa. 46. 3, 4). So that as God bade Israel to remember 'from Shittim unto Gilgal that ye may know the righteousness of the Lord' (Micah 6. 5), so would I persuade you, reader, to record the ways of Providence, from first to last, throughout your whole

[85]

course to this day, that you may see what a God He has been to you.

The seasonableness and opportuneness of its provisions for them, for so runs the promise : 'When the poor and needy seek water, and there is none, and their tongue faileth for thirst, I the Lord will hear them, I the God of Israel will not forsake them' (Isa. 41. 17), and so has the performance of it been. And this has been made good to distressed saints sometimes in a more ordinary way, God secretly blessing a little, and making it sufficient for us and ours. Job tells us of 'when the secret of God was upon my tabernacle' (29. 4), i.e., his secret blessing is in their tabernacles. It is by reason of this that they subsist, but it is in an unaccountable way that they do so. And sometimes in an extraordinary way it breaks forth for their supply. So you find the cruse and barrel fail not (2 Kings 17. 9–14).

Samuel Clarke, in the life of that painstaking and humble servant of Christ, John Foxe, records a memorable instance of Providence, and it is this. Towards the end of King Henry VIII's reign he went to London, where he quickly spent what little his friends had given him, or he had acquired by his own diligence, and began to be in great want. As one day he sat in Paul's Church, spent with long fasting, his countenance thin and his eyes hollow, after the ghastly manner of dying men, every one shunning a spectacle of so much horror, there came to him one whom he had never seen before, who thrust an untold sum of money into his hand, bidding him be of good cheer and accept that small gift in good part from his country-man; and that he should make much of himself, for that within a few days new hopes were at hand, and a more certain condition of livelihood. Three days after, the duchess of Richmond sent for him to live in her house and be tutor to the earl of Surrey's children, then under her care.

Isaac Ambrose, a worthy divine, whose labours have made him acceptable to his generation, in his epistle to the Earl of Bedford, prefixed to his *Last Things*, gives a pregnant instance in his own experience. His words are these : 'For mine own part, however, the Lord has seen cause to give me but a poor

[86]

pittance of outward things, for which I bless His name; yet in the income thereof, I have many times observed so much of His peculiar providence, that thereby they have been very much sweetened, and my heart has been raised to admire His grace. When of late, under a hard dispensation, which I judge not meet to mention, in which I suffered conscientiously, all streams of wonted supplies being stopped, the waters of relief for myself and family did run low. I went to bed with some staggerings and doubtings of the fountain's letting out itself for our refreshing; but ere I did awake in the morning, a letter was brought to my bedside, which was signed by a choice friend, Mr Antony Ash, which reported some unexpected breakings out of God's goodness for my comfort.' These are some of his lines: 'Your God, who has given you a heart thankfully to record your experiences of His goodness, does renew experiences for your encouragement. Now I shall report one which will raise your spirit toward the God of your mercies.' Whereupon he sweetly concludes: 'One morsel of God's provision, especially when it comes in unexpected, and upon prayer, when wants are most, will be more sweet to a spiritual relish than all former enjoyments were.'

The wisdom of Providence in our provisions. And this is seen in proportioning the quantity, not satisfying our extravagant wishes, but answering our real needs; consulting our wants, not our wantonness. 'But my God shall supply all your need' (Phil. 4. 19), and this has exactly suited the wishes of the best and wisest men, who desired no more at His hand. So Jacob (Gen. 28. 20) and Agur (Prov. 30. 8, 9). Wise Providence considers our condition as pilgrims and strangers, and so allots the provision that is needful for our passage home. It knows the mischievous influence of fulness and excess upon most men, though sanctified, and how apt it is to make them remiss and forgetful of God (Deut. 6. 12) so that their heart, like the moon, suffers an eclipse when it is at the full; and so suits and orders all to their best advantage.

The wisdom of Providence is also greatly revealed in the manner of dispensing our portion to us. It many times allows our wants to pinch hard, and many fears to arise, with a design to magnify the care and love of God in the supply (Deut. 8. 3). Providence so orders the case, that faith and prayer come between our wants and supplies, and the goodness of God may be the more magnified in our eyes thereby.

And now let me beg you to consider the good hand of Providence that has provided for, and suitably supplied you and yours all your days, and never failed you hitherto. And labour to walk suitably to your experience of such mercies. That you may do this, let me press a few suitable cautions upon you.

Beware that you do not forget the care and kindness of Providence which your eyes have seen in so many fruits and experiences. It was God's charge against Israel 'that they soon forgat his works' (Ps. 106. 13). A bad heart and a slippery memory deprive men of the comfort of many mercies, and defraud God of the glory due for them.

Do not distrust Providence in future exigencies. Thus they did: 'Behold, he smote the rock, that the waters gushed out, and the streams overflowed; can he give bread also? can he provide flesh for his people?' (Ps. 78. 20). How unreasonable and absurd are these queries of unbelief, especially after their eyes had seen the power of God in such extraordinary works.

Do not murmur and complain under new straits. This is a vile temper, and yet how natural to us when wants press hard upon us! Ah, did we but rightly understand what the demerit of sin is, we would rather admire the bounty of God than complain of the straithandedness of Providence. And if we did but consider that there lies upon God no obligation of justice or gratitude to reward any of our duties, it would cure our murmurs (Gen. 32. 10).

Do not show the least discontent at the lot and portion Providence carves out for you. O that you would be well pleased and satisfied with all its appointments! Say: 'The lines are fallen unto me in pleasant places; yea, I have a goodly heritage' (Ps. 16. 6). Surely that is best for you which Providence has appointed, and one day you yourselves will judge it so to be.

Do not neglect prayer when straits befall you. You see it is Providence dispenses all, you live upon it; therefore apply yourselves to God in the times of need. This is evidently included in the promise (Isa. 41. 17) as well as expressed in the command (Phil. 4. 6). Remember God, and He will not forget you.

Do not worry your hearts with sinful cares. 'Behold the fowls of the air' (Matt. 6. 26), says Christ; not the fowls at the door that are daily fed by hand, but those of the air, that do not know where the next meal is coming from; and yet God provides for them. Remember your relation to Christ, and His engagements by promise to you, and by these things work your hearts to satisfaction and contentment with all the allotments of Providence.

6

PRESERVATION OF THE SAINTS
FROM EVIL

———

A further great advantage and mercy the saints receive from
the hand of Providence is in their preservation from the snares
and temptations of sin, by its preventing care over them. That
Providence wards off many a deadly stroke of temptation and
many a mortal thrust which Satan makes at our souls is a
truth as manifest as the light that shines. This is included in
that promise: God 'will with the temptation also make a
way to escape, that ye may be able to bear it' (1 Cor. 10. 13).
Providence gives an outlet for the soul's escape when it is shut
up in the dangerous straits of temptation. There are two
eminent ways by which the force and efficacy of temptation is
broken in believers. One is by the operation of internal grace.
'The flesh lusteth against the Spirit, and the Spirit against the
flesh; so that ye cannot do the things that ye would' (Gal. 5.
17), i.e., sanctification gives sin a miscarrying womb after it
has conceived in the soul. The other way is by the external
working of Providence; and of this I intend to speak here.

The Providence of God is the great barrier and hindrance to
a world of sin, which otherwise would break forth like an
overflowing flood from our corrupt natures. It prevents abundance of sin, which otherwise wicked men would commit
(Gen. 19. 11). The Sodomites were greedily pursuing their
lusts; God providentially hinders it by smiting them blind.
Jeroboam intends to smite the prophet; Providence interposed
and withered his arm (1 Kings 13. 4). Thus you see, when

wicked men have contrived and are ready to execute their wickedness, Providence claps on its manacles 'so that their hands cannot perform their enterprise' (Job 5. 12).

And so much corruption there remains in good men that they would certainly plunge themselves under much more guilt than they do if Providence did not take greater care of them than they do of themselves. For though they make conscience of keeping themselves, and daily watch their hearts and ways, yet such is the deceitfulness of sin that if Providence did not lay blocks in their way, it would, more frequently than it does, entangle and defile them. And this it does in several ways.

Sometimes by stirring up others to interpose with seasonable counsels, which effectually dissuade them from prosecuting an evil design. Thus Abigail meets David in the nick of time, and dissuades him from his evil purpose (1 Sam. 25. 34).

And I find it recorded, as on another account was noted before, of that holy man Mr Dod, that being late at night in his study, he was strongly moved, though at an unseasonable hour, to visit a gentleman of his acquaintance. Not knowing what might be the design of Providence in this, he obeyed and went. When he came to the house, after a few knocks on the door, the gentleman himself came to him and asked him whether he had any business with him. Mr Dod answered, No; but that he could not be quiet till he had seen him. O, Sir, replied the gentleman, you are sent of God at this hour, for just now (and with that takes the halter out of his pocket) I was going to destroy myself. And thus was the mischief prevented.

Sometimes by hindering the means and instruments, whereby the evil itself is prevented. Thus, when good Jehoshaphat had joined himself with that wicked King Ahaziah to build ships at Ezion-gaber to go to Tarshish, God prevents the design by breaking the ships with a storm (2 Chron. 20. 35–37).

We find also in the life of Mr Bolton, written by Mr Bagshaw, that while he was in Oxford he had familiar acquaintance with Mr Anderton, a good scholar, but a strong papist, who knowing Mr Bolton's natural gifts, and perceiving that he was in some outward need, took this advantage and used many arguments to persuade him to be reconciled to the Church of Rome, and to go over with him to the English seminary, assuring him he should be furnished with all necessities and have gold enough. Mr Bolton being at that time poor in mind and purse, accepted the invitation, and a day and place was appointed in Lancashire, where they should meet and take shipping and be gone. But Mr Anderton did not come, and so he escaped the snare.

Sometimes by laying some strong affliction upon the body, to prevent a worse evil. And this is the meaning of : 'I will hedge up thy way with thorns' (Hos. 2. 6). Thus Basil was a long time exercised with a violent headache which he observed was used by Providence to prevent lust. Paul had a thorn in the flesh, a messenger of Satan sent to buffet him; and this affliction, whatever it was, was ordained to prevent pride in him (2 Cor. 12. 7).

Sometimes sin is prevented in the saints *by the better information of their minds at the sacred oracles of God*. Thus, when sinful motions began to rise in Asaph's mind, from the prosperity of the wicked and his own afflicted state, and grew to such a height that he began to think all he had done in the way of religion was little better than lost labour, he is set right again, and the temptation dissolved, by going into the sanctuary, where God showed him how to take new measures of persons and things, to judge them by their ends and issues, not their present appearances (Ps. 73. 12, 13, 17).

And sometimes the Providence of God prevents the sins of His people *by removing them out of the way of temptations by death*. In this sense we may understand that text : 'The righteous is taken away from the evil to come' (Isa. 57. 1), the evil of sin as well as sufferings. When the Lord sees His people low-spirited and not able to grapple with strong trials and temptations which are drawing on, it is for them a merciful Providence to be released by death and set out of harm's way.

Now consider and admire the Providence of God, O ye

saints, who has had more care of your souls than ever you had of them. Had not the Providence of God thus wrought for you in a way of prevention, it may be you had this day been so many Magor Missabibs.* How was the heart of David melted under that preventing providence aforementioned (1 Sam. 25. 32–34). He blesses the Lord, the instrument and that counsel by which his soul was preserved from sin. Do but seriously think of a few particulars about this case.

Think how your corrupt natures have often impetuously hurried you on towards sin, so that all the inherent grace you had could not withstand its force, if Providence had not prevented it in some such way as you have heard. 'But every man is tempted when he is drawn away of his own lust, and enticed' (James 1. 14). You found yourselves but feathers in the wind of temptation.

How near you have been brought to the brink of sin, and yet saved by a merciful hand of Providence. May you not say with one: 'I was almost in all evil' (Prov. 5. 14), and 'My feet were almost gone; my steps had well nigh slipped' (Ps. 73. 2). O merciful Providence that stepped in so opportunely to your relief!

How many have been allowed to fall by the hand of temptations, to the reproach of religion and wounding of their own consciences, so far that they have never recovered their former peace again, but lived in the world devoid of comfort to their dying day!

How woeful your case had been if the Lord had not mercifully saved you from many thousand temptations that have assaulted you! I tell you, you cannot estimate the mercies you possess by means of such providences. Are your names sweet, and your consciences peaceful, two mercies as dear to you as your two eyes? Why surely you owe them, if not wholly yet in great measure, to the aids and assistances Providence has given you all along the way you have passed through the dangerous tempting world to this day.

Walk therefore suitably to this obligation of Providence

*See Jer. 20. 3–4.

[93]

also. And see that you thankfully own it. Do not impute your escapes from sin to accidents, or to your own watchfulness or wisdom.

See also that you do not tempt Providence on the other hand, by an irregular reliance upon its care over you, without taking all due care of yourselves. 'Keep yourselves in the love of God' (Jude 21); 'Keep thy heart with all diligence' (Prov. 4. 23). Though Providence keep you, yet it is in the way of your duty.

Thus you see what care Providence has had over your souls in preventing the spiritual dangers and miseries that otherwise would have befallen you in the way of temptations.

In the next place I will show you that it has been no less concerned about your bodies, and with great tenderness it has carried them in its arms through innumerable hazards and dangers also. 'He that keepeth Israel shall neither slumber nor sleep' (Ps. 121. 4); 'He is the preserver of men' (Job 7. 20). To display the glory of this Providence before you, let us take into consideration the perils into which the best of men sometimes fall, and the ways and means by which Providence preserves them in those dangers.

There are many hazards into which we are often cast in this world. The Apostle Paul gives us a general account of his dangers (2 Cor. 11. 26), and how great a wonder is it that our life has not been extinguished in some of those dangers we have been in!

Have not some of us fallen, and that often, into very dangerous sicknesses and diseases, in which we have approached to the very brink of the grave (Job 33. 18, 21, 28), and have or might have said with Hezekiah: 'I said in the cutting off of my days, I shall go to the gates of the grave: I am deprived of the residue of my years' (Isa. 38. 10)? Have we not often had the sentence of death in ourselves? and our bodies at that time been like a leaky ship in a storm, as one* aptly resembles it, that has taken in water on every side, till it was ready to sink?

---

* T. Goodwin in his *Aggravation of Sin against Mercy*.

Yet has God preserved, repaired and launched us out again as well as ever. O what a wonder is it that such a crazy body should be preserved so many years, and survive so many dangers! Surely it is not more wonderful to see a Venice-glass* pass from hand to hand in continual use for forty or fifty years, and still to remain whole, notwithstanding the many knocks and falls it has had. If you enjoy health, or recover from sicknesses, it is because he puts 'none of these diseases upon thee,' or because he is 'the Lord that healeth thee' (Exod. 15. 26).

How many deadly dangers has His hand rescued some of you from in those years of confusion and public calamity when the sword was bathed in blood and made horrid slaughter, when, it may be, your lives were often given you for a prey! This David put a special remark upon: 'O God the Lord, the strength of my salvation: thou hast covered my head in the day of battle' (Ps. 140. 7).

Beza, being in France in the first Civil War and there tossed up and down for two and twenty months, recorded six hundred deliverances from dangers in that space, for which he solemnly gave God thanks in his last testament. If the sword did not destroy you, it was because God did not give it a commission to do so.

Many of you have seen wonders of salvation upon the deeps, where the hand of God has been signally stretched forth for your rescue and deliverance. This is elegantly expressed in Psalm 107. 23–27 (which I have elsewhere † expounded at large), concerning which you may say in a proper sense what the Psalmist says metaphorically: 'If it had not been the Lord who was on our side, then the waters had overwhelmed us, the stream had gone over our soul' (Ps. 124. 1, 4). To see men that have spent so many years upon the seas,‡ where your lives have continually hung in suspense before you, attain to

---

* A glass cup or goblet of rare purity and extreme sensitiveness.
† See *The Seaman's Companion.*
‡ A large proportion of Flavel's congregation at Dartmouth would consist of seafaring people.

your years, when you could neither be reckoned among the living or the dead, as seamen are not, O what cause have you to adore your great Preserver! Many thousands of your companions are gone down, and you are yet here to praise the Lord among the living. You have bordered nearer to eternity all your days than others, and often been in eminent perils upon the seas. Surely these and so many salvations call aloud to you for most thankful acknowledgments.

What innumerable hazards and accidents, the least of which have cut off others, has God carried us all through! I think I may safely say your privative and positive mercies of this kind are more in number than the hairs of your heads. Many thousands of these dangers we never saw, nor were made particularly aware of, but though we did not see them, our God did, and brought us out of danger before He brought us into fear. Some have been evident to us, and those so remarkable that we cannot think or speak of them to this day, but our souls are freshly affected with those mercies.

It is recorded of our famous Jewel,* that about the beginning of Queen Mary's reign, the inquisition taking hold of him in Oxford, he fled to London by night; but providentially losing the road, he escaped the inquisitors who pursued him. However, he fell that night into another imminent hazard of life, for wandering up and down in the snow, he fainted and lay starving in the way, panting and labouring for life, at which time Latimer's servant found and saved him.

It would be easy to multiply examples of this kind; histories abound with them. But I think there are few of us but are furnished out of our own experience abundantly; so that I shall rather choose to press home the sense of these providences upon you, in order that you may make a suitable return to the God of your mercies for them, than add more instances of this kind. To this purpose I desire you seriously to weigh the following particulars.

Consider what you owe to Providence for your protec-

* John Jewel (1522–71), Bishop of Salisbury and author of the famous *Apology of the Church of England.*

tion, by which your life has been protracted unto this day, with the usefulness and comfort thereof. Look around in the world, and you may daily see some in every place who are objects of pity, bereaved by sad accidents of all the comforts of life, while in the meantime Providence has tenderly preserved you. 'He keepeth all his bones, not one of them is broken' (Ps. 34. 20). Is the elegant and comely structure of your body unspoiled, your members not deformed, or made so many seats of torment, neither the usefulness of any part deprived? Why, this is because Providence never left its hold of you since you came out of the womb, but with a watchful eye and tender hand has guarded you in every place, and kept you as its charge.

Consider how every member which has been so tenderly kept, has nevertheless been an instrument of sin against the Lord; and that not only in the days of your unregeneracy, when you yielded 'your members as instruments of unrighteousness unto sin' (Rom. 6. 13), but even since you gave them up in covenant unto the Lord as dedicated instruments to His service; and yet how tender has Providence been over them! You have often provoked Him to afflict you in every part, and lay penal evil upon every member that has been instrumental in moral evil. But O, how great have His compassions been towards you, and His patience how wonderful!

Consider what is the aim of Providence in all the tender care it has manifested for you. Why does it protect you so assiduously, and suffer no evil to befall you? Is it not that you should employ your bodies for God, and cheerfully apply yourselves to that service He has called you to? Doubtless this is the end and goal of these mercies; or else to what purpose are they afforded you? Your bodies are a part of Christ's purchase, as well as your souls (1 Cor. 6. 19). They are committed to the charge and tutelage of angels (Heb. 1. 14), who have performed many services for them. They are dedicated by yourselves to the Lord, and that upon the highest account (Rom. 12. 1). They have already been the subjects of many mercies in this world (Ps. 35. 10), and shall partake of singular glory and happiness in the world to come (Phil. 3. 21). And shall they not then be employed, yea, cheerfully worn out, in His service? How reasonable it is they should be so! Why are they so tenderly preserved by God, if they must not be used for God?

7

THE WORK OF SANCTIFICATION

There is an eminent favour Providence bestows on the saints, which has not yet been considered, and indeed is too little minded by us, and that is the aid and assistance it gives the people of God in the great work of mortification.

Mortification of our sinful affections and passions is one half of our sanctification: 'dead indeed unto sin, but alive unto God' (Rom. 6. 11). It is the great evidence of our interest in Christ (Rom. 6. 5–9; Gal. 5. 24). It is our safety in the hour of temptation. The corruptions in the world are through lust (2 Peter 1. 4). Our instrumental fitness for service depends much upon it (John 15. 2; 2 Tim. 2. 21). How great a service to our souls therefore must that be, by which this blessed work is carried on in them!

Now there are two means or instruments employed in this work. The Spirit, who effects it internally (Rom. 8. 13), and Providence, which assists it externally. The Spirit indeed is the principal agent, upon whose operation the success of this work depends, and all the providences in the world can never effect it without Him. But they are secondary and subordinate means, which, by the blessing of the Spirit upon them, have a great part in the work. How they are so serviceable to this end and purpose, I shall now explain.

The most wise God orders the dispensations of Providence in a blessed subordination to the work of His Spirit. There is a sweet harmony between them in their distinct workings. They all meet in that one blessed issue to which God has by the counsel of His will directed them (Rom. 8. 28; Eph. 1. 11). Hence it is that the Spirit is said to be in, and to order the motions of the wheels of Providence (Ezek. 1. 20), and so they move together by consent. Now one great part of the Spirit's internal work being to destroy sin in the people of God, see how conformable to His design external providences are steered and ordered in the following particulars.

There is in all the regenerate a strong propensity and inclination to sin, and in that lies a principal part of the power of sin. Of this Paul sadly complains: 'But I see another law in my members, warring against the law of my mind, and bringing me into captivity to the law of sin which is in my members' (Rom. 7. 23): and every believer daily finds it to his grief. O, it is hard to forbear those things that grieve God. God has made a hedge about us, and fenced us against sin by His laws; but there is a proneness in nature to break over the hedge, and that against the very opposition of the Spirit of God in us. Now see in this case the concurrence and assistance of Providence for the prevention of sin. As the Spirit internally resists those sinful inclinations, so Providence externally lays bars and blocks in our way to hinder and prevent sin (Job 33. 17–19; Hosea 2. 6; 2 Cor. 12. 7). There is many a bodily ailment inflicted on this very score, to be a clog to prevent sin. O bear them patiently upon this consideration. Basil was sorely grieved with an inveterate headache; he earnestly prayed it might be removed; God removed it. No sooner was he freed of this clog, but he felt the inordinate motions of lust, which made him pray for his headache again. So it might be with many of us, if our clogs were off.

At this point it may be asked whether it is proper for a gracious spirit to forbear sin because of the rod of affliction? He has surely higher motives and nobler principles than these. This is the attitude of a carnal and slavish spirit!

Indeed it is so when this is the sole or principal restraint from sin, when a man does not abhor sin because of the intrinsic filth, but only because of the troublesome consequences and effects. But this is vastly different from the case of the saints under sanctified afflictions; for as they have higher motives and nobler principles, so they have lower and natural feelings too; and these are, in their kind and place, very useful to them.

Besides, you must know that afflictions work in another way upon gracious hearts to restrain them from sin, or warn them against sin, than they do upon others. It is not so much the smart of the rod which they feel, as the token of God's displeasure, which frightens and scares them. 'Thou renewest thy witnesses against me' (Job 10. 17), and this is that which principally affects them. 'O Lord, rebuke me not in thine anger, neither chasten me in thy hot displeasure' (Ps. 6. 1). 'O Lord, correct me, but with judgment; not in thine anger, lest thou bring me to nothing' (Jer. 10. 24): and surely this is no low and common argument.

Notwithstanding this double fence of God's command and preventive afflictions, yet sin is too hard for the best of men; their corruptions carry them through all to sin. And when it is so, not only does the Spirit work internally, but Providence also works externally in order to subdue them. The ways of sin are not only made bitter to them by the remorse of conscience, but by those afflictive rods upon the outward man, with which God also follows it; and in both these respects I find that text expounded: 'Whoso breaketh an hedge, a serpent shall bite him' (Eccles. 10. 8). If, as some expound it, the hedge is the law of God, then the serpent is the remorse of conscience, and the sharp teeth of affliction, which he shall quickly feel, if he is one that belongs to God.

The design and aim of these afflictive providences is to purge and cleanse believers from that pollution into which temptations have plunged them. 'By this, therefore, shall the iniquity of Jacob be purged, and this is all the fruit to take away his sin' (Isa. 27. 9). To the same purpose is that place: 'Before I was afflicted I went astray; but now have I kept thy word' (Ps. 119. 67). These afflictions have the same use and end to our souls that frosty weather has upon those clothes that are laid out to be bleached; they alter the hue and make them whiter, which seems to be the allusion in those words: 'And some of them of understanding shall fall, to try them, and to purge, and to make them white' (Dan. 11. 35).

And here it may be queried upon what account afflictions are said to purge away the iniquities of the saints? Is it not unwarrantable and very dishonourable to Christ, to attribute to affliction that which is the peculiar honour of His blood?

It is confessed that the blood of Christ is the only fountain opened for sin, and that no afflictions, however many or strong or continual they are, can in themselves purge away the pollution of sin, as we see in wicked men who are afflicted, and afflicted, and again afflicted; and yet nevertheless sinful. And the torments of hell, however extreme, universal and continual they are, yet shall never fetch out the stain of one sin.

But it is still true that a sanctified affliction may, in the efficacy and virtue of Christ's blood, produce such blessed effects upon the soul. Though a cross without a Christ never did any man any good, yet thousands have been indebted to the cross, as it has wrought in the virtue of His death for their good. And this is the case with those souls that this discourse is concerned about.

We find the best hearts, if God bestow any comfortable enjoyment upon them, too apt to be over-heated in their affections towards it, and to be too much taken up with these outward comforts. This also shows the great power and strength of corruption in the people of God, and must by some means or other be mortified in them.

This was the case of Hezekiah whose heart was too much set upon his treasures; so that he could not hide a vainglorious disposition (Isa. 39. 2). Likewise good David (Ps. 30. 7) thought his mountain, that is, his kingdom and the splendour and glory of his present state, had stood so fast that it should never be moved.

How the same good man set his heart and affections upon his beautiful son Absalom appears by the doleful lamentation he made at his death, prizing him above his own life, which was a thousand times more worth than he.

So Jonah, when God raised up a gourd for him to shelter him from the sun, how excessively was he taken with it, and was exceedingly glad of it!

But will God allow things to lie thus? Shall the creature purloin and draw away our affections from Him? No, this is our corruption, and God will purge it. And to this end He sends forth Providence to smite those creatures on which our affections are either inordinately or excessively set, or else to turn them into rods, and smite us with them.

Is Hezekiah too much puffed up with his full exchequer? Why, those very Babylonians to whom he boasted of it, shall empty it and make a prey of it (Isa. 39. 6).

Is David hugging himself in a fond conceit of the stability of his earthly splendour? Lo! how soon God beclouds all (Ps. 30. 7). Is Absalom doted on, and crept too far into his good father's heart? This shall be the son of his sorrow, that shall seek after his father's life.

Is Jonah so carried away with his gourd? God will prepare a worm to smite it (4. 6, 7).

How many husbands, wives and children has Providence smitten for this very reason! It might have spared them longer, if they had been loved more regularly and moderately. This has blasted many an estate and hopeful project; and it is a merciful dispensation for our good.

The strength of our unmortified corruption shows itself in our pride and the swelling vanity of our hearts when we have a name and esteem among men. When we are applauded and honoured, when we are admired for any gift or excellence that is in us, this draws forth the pride of the heart and shows the vanity that is in it. 'As the fining pot for silver, and the furnace for gold; so is a man to his praise' (Prov. 27. 21); i.e., as the furnace will reveal what dross is in the metal when it is melted, so will praise and commendations reveal what pride is in the heart of him that receives them. This made a good man say: 'He that praises me, wounds me.' And, which is more strange, this corruption may be felt in the heart, even when the last breath is ready to expire. It was the saying of one of the German divines, when those about him recounted for his encouragement the many services he had done for God, 'Take away the fire, for there is still the chaff of pride in me.' To crucify this corruption Providence takes off the bridle of restraint from ungodly men, and sometimes permits them to traduce the names of God's servants, as Shimei did David's. Yea, they shall fall into disesteem among their friends, as Paul did among the Corinthians; and all this to keep down the swelling of their spirits at the realization of those excellences that are in them. The design of these providences is nothing else but to hide pride from man. Yea, it deserves a special remark, that when some good men have been engaged in a public and eminent work, and have therein, it may be, too much sought their own applause, God has withheld His usual assistance at such times from them, and caused them so to falter in their work, that they have come off with shame and pity at such times, however ready and prepared they have been at other times. It would be easy to give various remarkable examples to confirm this observation, but I pass on.

The corruption of the heart shows itself in raising up great expectations to ourselves from the creature, and planning abundance of felicity and contentment from some promising and hopeful enjoyments we have in the world. This we find to have been the case of holy Job in the days of his prosperity: 'Then I said, I shall die in my nest, and I shall multiply my days as the sand' (29. 18). But how soon were all these expectations dashed by a gloomy Providence, that benighted him in the noontide of his prosperity. And all this was for his good, to take off his heart more fully from creature expectations. We often find the best men over-reckon themselves in worldly things, and overact their confidences about them. They that have great and well-grounded expectations from heaven, may have too great and ungrounded expectations from the earth. But when it is so, it is very usual for Providence to undermine their earthly hopes, and convince them by experience how vain they are. Thus, in Haggai 1. 9, the people's hearts were intently set upon prosperous providences, full harvests and great increase; while in the meantime no regard was had to the worship of God and the things of His house; therefore Providence blasts their hopes and brings them to little.

Corruption shows itself in dependence upon creature-comforts and tangible props. O how apt are the best of men to lean upon these things, and stay themselves upon them! Thus did Israel stay themselves upon Egypt, as a feeble man would lean upon his staff; but God allowed it both to fail them and wound them (Ezek. 29. 6–7). So for individuals, how apt are they to depend upon their tangible supports! Thus we lean on our relations, and the inward thoughts of our hearts are that they shall be to us so many springs of comfort to refresh us throughout our lives; but God will show us by His Providence our mistake and error in these things. Thus a husband is smitten, to draw the soul of a wife nearer to God in dependence upon Him (1 Tim. 5. 5). So for children, we are apt to say of this or that child, as Lamech of Noah, 'This same shall comfort us' (Gen. 5. 29); but the wind passes over these flowers and they are withered, to teach us that our happiness is not bound up in these enjoyments. So for our estates, when the world smiles upon us, and we have got a warm nest, how do we prophesy of rest and peace in those acquisitions, thinking, with good Baruch, great things for ourselves; but Providence by a particular or general calamity overturns our plans (Jer. 45. 4, 5), and all this to turn our hearts from the creature to God, who is our only rest.

Corruption shows its strength in good men by their adherence to things below and their reluctance to go hence. This often proceeds from the engaging enjoyments and pleasant experiences we have here below. Providence mortifies this inclination in the saints by killing those ensnaring comforts beforehand, making all or most of our pleasant things to die before us. Or it embitters this world to us, by the troubles of it, making life undesirable, through the pains and infirmities we feel in the body, and so loosing our root for our more easy fall by the fatal stroke.

Before I pass from this, I cannot but make a pause, and desire you with me to stand in holy amazement and wonder at the dealings of God with such poor worms as we are. Surely God deals familiarly with men; His condescensions to His own clay are astonishing. All that I shall note at present about it shall be under these three heads, in which I find the matter of my present meditations summed up by the Psalmist : 'Lord, what is man, that thou takest knowledge of him, or the son of man that thou makest account of him!' (144. 3). In this Scripture you have represented the immense and transcendent greatness of God, who is infinitely above us and all our thoughts. 'Canst thou by searching find out God? canst thou find out the Almighty unto perfection? It is as high as heaven; what canst thou do? deeper than hell; what canst thou know? The measure thereof is longer than the earth, and broader than the sea' (Job 11. 7–9). 'The heaven and heaven of heavens cannot contain him' (2 Chron. 2. 6). He is 'glorious in holiness, fearful in praises, doing wonders' (Exod. 15. 11). When the Scripture speaks of Him comparatively, see how it expresses His greatness : 'Behold, the nations are as the drop of a bucket, and are counted as the small dust of the balance : behold, he taketh up the isles as a very little thing. And Lebanon is not sufficient to burn, nor the beasts thereof sufficient for a burnt offering. All nations before him are as nothing; and they are accounted to him less than nothing, and vanity (Isa. 40. 15–17). When the holiest men have addressed Him, see with what humility and deep adoration they have spoken of Him and to Him! 'Woe is me! for I am undone; because I am a man of unclean lips, and I dwell in the midst of a people of unclean lips; for mine eyes have seen the King, the Lord of hosts' (Isa. 6. 5). Nay, what respects the very angels of heaven have of that glorious Majesty : 'Each one had six wings; with twain he covered his face, and with twain he covered his feet, and with twain he did fly. And one cried unto another, and said : Holy, holy, holy, is the Lord of hosts; the whole earth is full of his glory' (verses 2 and 3).

Secondly, you have the baseness, vileness and utter un-worthiness of man, yea, the holiest and best of men, before God: 'Verily every man at his best state is altogether vanity' (Ps. 39. 5). 'Every man,' take where you will; and every man 'in his best state,' or 'standing in his freshest glory,' is not only 'vanity,' but 'altogether vanity,' literally 'every man is very vanity.' For do but consider the best of men in their extraction. 'By nature the children of wrath even as others' (Eph. 2. 3). The blood that runs in our veins is as much tainted as theirs in hell.

Consider them in their constitution and natural disposition, and it is no better, yea, in many there is worse disposition than in reprobates. And though grace depose sin in them from the throne, yet, O what offensive and God-provoking corruptions daily break out of the best hearts.

Consider them in their outward condition, and they are inferior, for the most part, to others. 'I thank thee, O Father, Lord of heaven and earth, because thou hast hid these things from the wise and prudent, and hast revealed them unto babes' (Matt. 11. 25; cf. 1 Cor. 1. 26–28).

And now let us consider and marvel that ever this great and blessed God should be so much concerned, as you have heard He is in all His providences, about such vile, despicable worms as we are! He does not need us, but is perfectly blessed and happy in Himself without us. We can add nothing to Him: 'Can a man be profitable unto God?' (Job 22. 2). No, the holiest of men add nothing to Him; yet, see how great account He makes of us. For does not His eternal electing love show the dear account He made of us (Eph. 1. 4, 5)? How ancient, how free, and how astonishing is this act of grace! This is that design which all providences are in pursuit of, and will not rest till they have executed.

Does not the gift of His only Son out of His bosom show this, that God makes great account of this vile thing, man? Never was man so magnified before. If David could say: 'When I consider thy heavens, the work of thy fingers, the

moon and the stars which thou hast ordained; what is man?'
(Ps. 8. 3, 4), how much more may we say, 'When we consider
Thy Son, that lay in Thy bosom, His infinite excellence and
unspeakable dearness to Thee, Lord, what is man, that such a
Christ should be delivered to death for him! for him, and not
for fallen angels (Heb. 2. 16), for him when in a state of enmity
with God (Rom. 5. 8).

Does not the assiduity of His providential care for us show
His esteem of us? 'Lest any hurt it, I will keep it night and
day' (Isa. 27. 3). 'He withdraweth not his eyes from the
righteous' (Job. 36. 7), no, not a moment all their days; for if
He did, a thousand mischiefs in that moment would rush in
upon them and ruin them.

Does not the tenderness of His providence show His esteem
of us? 'As one whom his mother comforteth, so will I comfort you' (Isa. 66. 13). He comforts His own by refreshing providences, as an indulgent mother her tender child. 'As birds flying' (Isa. 31. 5), viz., to their nests when their young are in
danger, so He defends His. No parental tenderness in the
creature can shadow forth the tender affection of the Creator.

Does not the variety of the fruits of His providence show
it? Our mercies are 'new every morning' (cf. Ps. 40. 5;
Lam. 3. 23). It is a fountain from which do stream forth
spiritual and temporal, ordinary and extraordinary, public and
personal mercies, mercies without number.

Does not the ministry of angels in the providential kingdom
show it? 'Are they not all ministering spirits sent forth to
minister for them who shall be heirs of salvation?' (Heb. 1. 14).

Does not the providence of which this day* calls us to cele-
brate the memory, show the great regard God has for His
people? O if not so, why were we not given up 'as a prey to
their teeth?' 'If it had not been the Lord who was on our side,'
then wicked men, compared to fire, water, wild beasts, 'had
swallowed us up quick' (Ps. 124). O blessed be God for that
teeming providence that has already brought forth more than

* Preached November 5.

seventy years liberty and peace to the Church of God. I suggest concerning this providence that you do by it as the Jews by their Purim (Esth. 9. 27, 28), and the rather, because we seem now to be as near danger by the same enemy as ever since that time. If such a mercy as this is forgotten, God may say: 'I will deliver you no more' (Judges 10. 13).

II

MEDITATION
ON THE PROVIDENCE
OF GOD

8

THE DUTY OF MEDITATION ON PROVIDENCE

Having proved the affairs of the people of God to be conducted by the care of special Providence, and given instances
of what influence Providence has upon those interests and
concerns of theirs, we come in the next place to prove it to
be the duty of the people of God to meditate upon these performances of Providence for them, at all times, but especially
in times of difficulty and trouble.

This is our duty *because God has expressly commanded it*,
and called His people to make the most serious reflections
upon His works, whether of mercy or judgment. So when
that most dreadful of all judgments was executed upon His
professing people for their apostasy from God, and God had
removed the symbols of His presence from among them, the
rest are bidden to go, that is, by their meditations, to send at
least their thoughts to Shiloh, and see what God did to it
(Jer. 7. 12). So for mercies, God calls us to consider and review
them. 'O my people, remember now what Balak king of Moab
consulted, and what Balaam the son of Beor answered him
from Shittim unto Gilgal; that ye may know the righteousness
of the Lord' (Mic. 6. 5). As much as to say, if you do not reflect
upon that signal providence, my righteousness will be covered,
and your unrighteousness uncovered. So for God's works of
providence concerning the creatures, we are called to consider
them, that we may prop up our faith by those considerations
for our own supplies (Matt. 6. 28).

It is plain that this is our duty *because the neglect of it is everywhere in Scripture condemned as a sin.* To be careless and unobservant is very displeasing to God, and so much appears by that Scripture: 'Lord, when thy hand is lifted up they will not see' (Isa. 26. 11). Nay, it is a sin which God threatens and denounces woe against in His Word (Ps. 28. 4, 5; Isa. 5. 12, 13). Yea, God not only threatens, but smites men with visible judgments for this sin (Job. 34. 26, 27).

And for this end and purpose it is that the Holy Ghost has affixed notes of attention such as 'behold' to the narratives of the works of providence in Scripture. All these invite and call men to a due and deep observation of them. For example, in that great and celebrated work of Providence in delivering Israel out of Egyptian bondage, you find a note of attention twice affixed to it (Exod. 3. 2, 9). Again, when that daring enemy Rabshakeh that put Hezekiah and all the people into such a consternation was defeated by Providence, there is a note of attention prefixed to that providence, 'Behold, I will send a blast upon him' (2 Kings 19. 7). When God glorifies His wisdom and power in delivering His people from their enemies, and ensnaring the latter in the works of their own hands, a double note of attention is affixed to that double work of Providence: 'Higgaion selah' (Ps. 9. 16). Also at the opening of every seal which contains a remarkable series or branch of Providence, how particularly is attention commanded to every one of them: 'Come and see, come and see' (Rev. 6. 1–7). All these are very useless and superfluous additions in Scripture, if no such duty lies upon us (see Ps. 66. 5).

Without due observation of the works of Providence no praise can be rendered to God for any of them. Praise and thanksgiving for mercies depend upon this act of observation of them, and cannot be performed without it. Psalm 107 is spent in narrating God's providential care of men: to His people in difficulties (4–6); to prisoners in their bonds (10–12); to men that lie languishing upon beds of sickness (17–19); to seamen upon the stormy ocean (23); to men in times of famine (33–40). Yea, His providence is displayed in all those changes that occur in the world, debasing the high, and exalting the low (40–41), and at every paragraph men are called upon to praise God for each of these providences. Verse 43 shows you what a necessary ingredient to that duty observation is: 'Whoso is wise, and will observe these things, even they shall understand the lovingkindness of the Lord.' So that of necessity, God must be defrauded of His praise if this duty is neglected.

Without this we lose the usefulness and benefit of all the works of God for us or others, which would be an unspeakable loss indeed to us. This is the food our faith lives upon in days of distress: 'Thou brakest the heads of leviathan in pieces, and gavest him to be meat to the people inhabiting the wilderness' (Ps. 74. 14), i.e., food to their faith. From providences past saints argue to fresh and new ones to come. So David: 'The Lord that delivered me out of the paw of the lion, and out of the paw of the bear, he will deliver me out of the hand of this Philistine' (1 Sam. 17. 37). So Paul: 'Who hath delivered, and in whom also we trust that he will yet deliver' (2 Cor. 1. 10). If these are forgotten or not considered, the hands of faith hang down. 'How is it that ye do not remember, neither consider?' (Matt. 16. 9). This is a topic from which the saints have often drawn their arguments in prayer for new mercies. As when Moses prays for continued or new pardons for the people, he argues from what was past: 'As thou hast forgiven them from Egypt until now' (Num. 14. 19); so the Church argues for new providences upon the same ground Moses pleaded for new pardons (Isa. 51. 9, 10).

It is a vile slighting of God not to observe what He manifests of Himself in His providences. For in all providences, especially in some, He comes near to us. He does so in His judgments: 'I will come near to you in judgment' (Mal. 3. 5). He comes near in mercies also: 'The Lord is nigh unto all them that call upon him' (Ps. 145. 18). Yea, He is said to visit us by His providence when He corrects (Hos. 9. 7), and when He saves and delivers (Ps. 106. 4). These visitations of God preserve our spirits (Job 10. 12), and it is a wonderful condescension in the great God to visit us so often, 'every morning and . . . every moment' (Job 7. 18). But not to take notice of it is a vile and brutish contempt of God (Isa. 1. 3; Zeph. 3. 2). You would not do so to a man for whom you have any respect. It is the character of the wicked not to regard God's favours (Isa. 26. 10) or frowns (Jer. 5. 3).

In a word, *men can never order their addresses to God in prayer, suitable to their conditions, without due observation of His providences.* Your prayers are to be suitable to your conditions: sometimes we are called to praise, sometimes to humiliation. In the way of His judgments you are to wait for Him (Isa. 26. 8), to prepare to meet him (Zeph. 2. 1, 2; Amos 4. 12). Sometimes your business is to turn away His anger which you see approaching, and sometimes you are called to praise Him for mercies received (Isa. 12. 1, 2), but then you must first observe them.

Thus you find the matter of David's psalms still varied, according to the providences that befell him: but one who is unobservant and careless can never do it. And thus you have the grounds of the duty briefly presented.

9

HOW TO MEDITATE ON THE
PROVIDENCE OF GOD

───────

Next we proceed to show in what manner we are to reflect upon the performances of Providence for us. And certainly, it is not every slight and transient glance, nor every cold, historical, unaffecting rehearsal or recognition of His providences towards you that will pass with God for a discharge of this great duty. No, no, it is another kind of work than what most men understand it to be. O that we were but acquainted with this heavenly spiritual exercise, how sweet it would make our lives, how light it would make our burdens! Ah, sirs, you live estranged from the pleasure of the Christian life, while you live in the ignorance or neglect of this duty. Now to lead you up to this heavenly, sweet and profitable exercise, I will beg your attention to the following directions:

Labour to get as full and thorough a recognition as you are able of the providences of God concerning you from first to last.

O fill your hearts with the thoughts of Him and His ways. If a single act of Providence is so ravishing and transporting, what would many such be, if they were presented together to the view of the soul! If one star is so beautiful to behold, what is a constellation! Let your reflections therefore upon the acts and workings of Providence for you be full, extensively and intensively.

Let them be as extensively full as may be. Search backward

into all the performances of Providence throughout your lives. So did Asaph: 'I will remember the works of the Lord: surely I will remember thy wonders of old. I will meditate also of all thy work, and talk of thy doings' (Ps. 77. 11, 12). He laboured to recover and revive the ancient providences of God's mercies many years past, and suck a fresh sweetness out of them by new reviews of them. Ah, sirs, let me tell you, there is not such a pleasant history for you to read in all the world as the history of your own lives, if you would but sit down and record from the beginning hitherto what God has been to you, and done for you; what signal manifestations and outbreakings of His mercy, faithfulness and love there have been in all the conditions you have passed through. If your hearts do not melt before you have gone half through that history, they are hard hearts indeed. 'My Father, thou art the guide of my youth' (Jer. 3. 4).

Let your meditation be as intensively full as may be. Do not let your thoughts swim like feathers upon the surface of the waters, but sink like lead to the bottom. 'The works of the Lord are great, sought out of them that have pleasure therein' (Ps. 111. 2). Not that I think it feasible to sound the depth of Providence by our short line: 'Thy way is in the sea, and thy path in the great waters, and thy footsteps are not known' (Ps. 77. 19), but it is our duty to dive as far as we can; and to admire the depth, when we cannot touch the bottom. It is in our viewing providences as it was with Elijah's servant, when he looked out for rain (1 Kings 18. 44); he went out once and viewed the heavens, and saw nothing, but the prophet bids him go again and again, and look upon the face of heaven seven times; and when he had done so, what now, says the prophet? 'O now', says he: 'I see a cloud rising like a man's hand'; and then, keeping his eye intently upon it, he sees the whole face of heaven covered with clouds. So you may look upon some providences once and again, and see little or nothing in them; but look 'seven times', that is, meditate often upon them, and you will see their increasing glory, like that increasing cloud.

There are several things to be distinctly pondered, and valued in one single providence, before you can judge the amount and worth of it. First, the seasonableness of mercy may give it a very great value. That it is timed so opportunely, and occurs just when needed, makes it a thousand-fold more considerable to you than the same mercy would have been at another time. Thus when our needs are permitted to grow to an extremity, and all visible hopes fail, then to have relief given wonderfully enhances the price of such a mercy (Isa. 41. 17, 18).

The peculiar care and kindness of Providence to us is a consideration which exceedingly heightens the mercy in itself, and endears it to us. So when, in general calamities upon the world, we are exempted by the favour of Providence, covered under its wings; when God shall call to us in evil days : 'Come, my people, enter thou into thy chambers' (Isa. 26. 20); when such promises shall be fulfilled to us in times of want or famine (Ps. 33. 18, 19); when others are abandoned and exposed to misery who have every way as much, it may be much more, visible security against it, and yet they are delivered up and we saved – O how endearing are such providences! (Ps. 91. 7, 8).

What a providence introduces is of special regard and consideration, and by no means to be neglected by us. There are leading providences which, however slight and trivial they may seem in themselves, yet in this respect justly challenge the first rank among providential favours to us because they usher in a multitude of other mercies, and draw a blessed train of happy consequences after them. Such a providence was that of Jesse's sending David with provisions to his brethren that lay encamped in the army (1 Sam. 17. 17). And thus every Christian may furnish himself out of his own stock of experience, if he will but reflect and consider the place where he is, the relations that he has, and the way by which he was led into them.

The instruments employed by Providence for you are of special consideration, and the finger of God is clearly seen by us when we pursue that meditation. For sometimes great mercies are conveyed to us by very improbable means, and more probable ones laid aside. A stranger is stirred up to do that for you which your near relations in nature had no power or will to do for you. Jonathan, a mere stranger to David, clave closer to him, and was more friendly and useful to him than his own brethren, who despised and slighted him. Ministers have found more kindness and respect from strangers than from their own people that are more obliged to them. 'A prophet,' said Christ, 'is not without honour, but in his own country, and among his own kin, and in his own house' (Mark 6. 4).

Sometimes help has come from the hands of enemies, as well as strangers: 'The earth helped the woman' (Rev. 12, 16.) God has bowed the hearts of many wicked men to show great kindness to His people (Acts 28. 2).

Sometimes God makes use of instruments for good to His people, who designed nothing but evil and mischief to them. Thus Joseph's brethren were instrumental to his advancement in that very thing in which they designed his ruin (Gen. 50. 20).

The design and scope of Providence must not escape our thorough consideration, what the aim and goal of Providence is. And truly this, of all others, is the most warming and melting consideration. You have the general account of the aim of all providences: 'And we know that all things work together for good to them that love God, to them who are the called according to his purpose' (Rom. 8. 28). A thousand friendly hands are at work for them, to promote and bring about their happiness. O this is enough to sweeten the bitterest providence to us, that we know it shall turn to our salvation (Phil. 1. 19).

The respect and relation Providence bears to our prayers is of singular consideration, and a most taking and sweet meditation. Prayer honours Providence, and Providence honours prayer. Great notice is taken of this in Scripture (Gen. 24. 45; Dan. 9. 20; Acts 12. 12). You have had the very petitions you asked of Him. Providences have borne the very signatures of your prayers upon them. O how affectingly sweet are such mercies!

In all your observations of Providence have special respect to that Word of God which is fulfilled and made good to you by them.

This is a clear truth that all providences have relation to the written Word. Thus Solomon in his prayer acknowledges that the promises and providences of God went along step by step with his father David all his days; and that His hand (put there for his Providence) had fulfilled whatever His mouth had spoken (1 Kings 8. 24). So Joshua in like manner acknowledges that 'not one good thing had failed of all the good things of which the Lord had spoken' (Josh. 22. 14). He had carefully observed what relation the works of God had to His Word. He compared them together, and found an exact harmony. And so may you too, if you will compare them as he did.

This I shall the more insist upon because it is by some interpreters supposed to be the very scope of the text. For (as was noted in the explanation) they supply and fill the sense with 'the things which He has promised,' and so read the text thus: 'I will cry unto God most high; unto God that performeth the things He has promised for me' (Ps. 57. 2).

Now, though I see no reason to limit the sense so narrowly, yet it cannot be denied that this is an especial part of its meaning. Let us therefore in all our reviews of Providence consider what Word of God, whether it be of threatening, caution, counsel or promise, is at any time made good to us by His providences.

Doing this will greatly confirm to us the truth of the Scripture, when we see its truth so manifest in the events. Had Scripture no other seal or attestation, this alone would be an unanswerable argument of its divinity when men shall find in all ages the works of God wrought so exactly according to this model that we may say : 'As we have read or heard, so have we seen.' O how great a confirmation is here before our eyes!

Again, doing this will abundantly direct and instruct us in our present duties under all providences. We shall know what we have to do, and how to behave under all changes of conditions. You can learn the voice and errand of the rod only from the Word (Ps. 94. 12) which interprets the works of God. Providences in themselves are not a perfect guide. They often puzzle and entangle our thoughts; but bring them to the Word, and your duty will be quickly manifested. 'Until I went into the sanctuary of God, then understood I their end' (Ps. 73. 17). And not only their end, but his own duty, to be quiet in an afflicted condition and not envy their prosperity.

Well then, bring those providences you have passed through, or are now under, to the Word, and you will find yourselves surrounded with a marvellous light, and see the verification of the Scriptures in them. I shall therefore here appeal to your consciences whether you have not found these events of Providence occurring agreeably in all respects with the Word.

The Word tells you that it is your wisdom and interest to keep close to its rules and the duties it prescribes. It tells that the way of holiness and obedience is the wisest way. 'This is your wisdom' (Deut. 4. 5, 6).

Now, let the events of Providence speak, whether this is true or not. Certainly it will appear to be so, whether we respect our present comfort or future happiness, both which we may see daily exposed by departure from duty, and secured by keeping close to it. Let the question be asked of the drunk-ard, adulterer or profane swearer, when by sin they have ruined body, soul, estate and name, whether it be their wisdom to walk in those forbidden paths after their own lusts; whether they had not better consulted their own interest and comfort in keeping within the bounds and limits of God's commands? and they cannot but confess that 'this their way is their folly.' 'What fruit,' says the Apostle, 'had ye in those things whereof ye are now ashamed? for the end of those things is death' (Rom. 6. 21). Does not the Providence of God verify upon them those threatenings that are written in the experience of all ages? (Job 31. 12; Prov. 5. 9, 10; 23. 21, 29) all which woes and miseries they escape that walk in God's statutes. Look upon the ruined estates and bodies you may everywhere see, and behold the truth of the Scriptures evidently made good in those sad providences.

The Word tells you that your departure from the way of integrity and simplicity, to make use of sinful policies, shall never profit you (1 Sam. 12. 21; Prov. 3. 5).

Let the events of Providence speak regarding this also. Ask your own experience, and you shall have a full confirmation of this truth. Did you ever leave the way of simplicity and integrity, and use sinful shifts to bring about your own designs, and prosper in that way? Certainly God has cursed all the ways of sin; and whoever find they thrive with them, His people shall not. Israel would not rely upon the Lord, but trust in the shadow of Egypt, and what advantage had they by this sinful policy (Isa. 30. 1–5)? David used a great deal of sinful policy to cover his wicked deed, but did it prosper (2 Sam. 12. 12)? It is an excellent observation of Livy, 'Sinful policies in their first appearances are pleasant and promising, in their management difficult, in their event sad.' Some by sinful ways have obtained wealth, but that Scripture has been verified in their experience, 'Treasures of wickedness profit nothing' (Prov. 10. 2). Either God has blown upon it by a secret curse that it has done them no good, or given them such disquietness in their consciences that they have been forced to vomit it up ere they could find peace (Job 11. 13–15).

That which David gave as a charge to Solomon has been found experimentally true by thousands (1 Chron. 22. 12, 13), that the true way to prosperity is to keep close to the rule of the Word, and that the true reason why men cannot prosper is their forsaking that rule (2 Chron. 24. 20).

It is true, if God has a purpose to destroy a man, he may for a time permit him to succeed and prosper in his sin, for his greater hardening (Job 12. 6). But it is not so with those whom the Lord loves. Their sinful shifts shall never thrive with them.

The Word prohibits your trust and confidence in the creature, even the greatest and most powerful among creatures (Ps. 146. 3). It tells us that it is better to trust in the Lord than in them (Ps. 118. 8). It forbids our confidence in those creatures that are most nearly allied and related in the bonds of nature to us (Mic. 7. 5). It curses the man that gives to the creature that reliance which is due to God (Jer. 17. 5).

Consult the events of Providence in this case, and see whether the Word is not verified in it. Did you ever lean upon an Egyptian reed, and it did not break under you and pierce as well as deceive you? O, how often has this been evident in our experience! Whatsoever we have over-loved, idolized, and leaned upon, God has from time to time broken it, and made us to see the vanity of it; so that we find the readiest course to be rid of our comforts is to set our hearts inordinately or immoderately upon them. For our God is a jealous God, and will not part with His glory to another. The world is full of examples of persons deprived of their comforts, husbands, wives, children and estates for this reason, and by this means. If Jonah is overjoyed in his gourd, a worm is at once prepared to smite it. Hence it is that so many graves are opened for the burying of our idols out of our sight. If David says: 'My mountain shall stand strong, I shall not be moved,' the next news he shall hear is of darkness and trouble (Ps. 30. 6, 7). O how true and faithful do we find these sayings of God to be! Who cannot put to his seal and say: 'Thy Word is truth' (John 17. 17)?

The Word assures us that sin is the cause and inlet of affliction and sorrow, and that there is an inseparable connection between them. 'Be sure your sin will find you out' (Num. 32. 23); that is, the sad effects and afflictions that follow it shall find you out. 'If his children forsake my law and walk not in my judgments: if they break my statutes and keep not my commandments: then will I visit their transgression with the rod and their iniquities with stripes' (Ps. 89. 30–32).

Enquire now at the mouth of Providence whether this is indeed so, according to the reports of the Word. Ask but your own experiences, and you will find that just so Providence has ordered it all along your way. When did you grow into a secure, vain, carnal frame, but you found some rousing, startling providence sent to awaken you? When did you wound your consciences with guilt, and God did not wound you for it in some or other of your beloved enjoyments? Nay, so ordinary is this with God that from the observations of their own frames and ways many Christians have foreboded and presaged troubles at hand.

I do not say that God never afflicts His people but for their sin; for He may do it for their trial (1 Pet. 4. 12). Nor do I say that God follows every sin with a rod; for who then could stand before Him (Ps. 130. 3)? But this I say, that it is God's usual way to visit the sins of His people with rods of affliction, and this in mercy to their souls. For this reason it was that the rod of God was upon David in a long succession of troubles upon his kingdom and family, after that great prevarication of his (2 Sam. 12. 10). And if we would carefully search out the seeds and principles of those miseries under which we or ours do groan, we should find them to be our own turnings aside from the Lord (Jer. 2. 19; 4. 18). Have not all these cautions and threatenings of the Word been exactly fulfilled by Providence in your own experience? Who can but see the infallible truth of God in all that he has threatened!

And no less evident is the truth of the promises to all that will observe how Providence makes them good every day to us; for consider how great security God has given to His people in the promises, that no man shall lose anything by self-denial for His sake. He has told us, 'Verily, I say unto you : There is no man that hath left house, or brethren, or sisters, or father, or mother, or wife, or children, or lands, for my sake and the gospel's; but he shall receive an hundredfold now in this time, houses, and brethren, and sisters, and mothers, and children, and lands, with persecutions, and in the world to come, eternal life' (Mark 10. 29, 30).

Though that vile apostate Julian derided this promise, yet thousands and ten thousands have experienced it, and do at this day stand ready to set their seal to it. God has made it good to His people, not only in spiritual things, inward joy and peace, but even in temporal things also. Instead of natural relations, who took care for them before, hundreds of Christians shall stand ready to assist and help them, so that though they have left all for Christ, yet they may say with the apostle: 'As having nothing, and yet possessing all things' (2 Cor. 6. 10). O the admirable care and tenderness of Providence over those that for conscience sake have left all and cast themselves upon its immediate care! Are there not at this day to be found many so provided for, even to the envy of their enemies and their own admiration? Who does not see the faithfulness of God in the promises that has but a heart to trust God in them!

The Word of promise assures us that whatever wants or straits the saints fall into, their God will never leave them nor forsake them (Heb. 13. 5), that He 'will be with them in trouble' (Ps. 91. 15).

Consult the various providences of your life in this point, and I doubt not but you will find the truth of these promises as often confirmed as you have been in trouble. Ask your own hearts, where or when was it that your God forsook you, and left you to sink and perish under your burdens? I doubt not but most of you have been at one time or other plunged in difficulties, difficulties out of which you could see no way of escape by the eye of reason; yea, such as it may be staggered your faith in the promise, as David's was when he said, 'I shall now perish one day by the hand of Saul' (1 Sam. 27. 1). 'All men are liars' (Ps. 116. 11), even Samuel himself! And yet notwithstanding all, we see him emerge out of that sea of trouble, and the promises made good in every tittle to him. The like, doubtless, you may observe in your own case. Ask your own souls the question, and they will satisfy it. Did God abandon and cast you off in the day of trouble? Certainly you must belie your own experience if you should say so. It is true, there have been some plunges and difficulties you have met with, in which you could see no way of escape, but concluded you must perish in them. There have been difficulties that have staggered your faith in the promises, and made you doubt whether the fountain of all-sufficiency would let out itself for your relief; yea, such difficulties as have provoked you to murmuring and impatience, and thereby provoked the Lord to forsake you in your trouble; but yet you see He did not. He has either strengthened your back to bear, or lightened your burden, or else opened an unexpected door of escape, according to promise (1 Cor. 10. 13), so that the evil which you feared did not come upon you.

You read that the Word of God is the only support and relief to a gracious soul in the dark day of affliction (Ps. 119. 50, 92; 2 Sam. 23. 5), and that for this purpose it was written (Rom. 15. 4). No rules of moral prudence, no natural remedies can perform for us that which the Word can do.

And is not this a sealed truth attested by a thousand undeniable experiences? From this source have the saints fetched their cordials when fainting under the rod. One word of God can do more than ten thousand words of men to relieve a distressed soul. If Providence has at any time directed you to such promises as either assure you that the Lord will be with you in trouble (Ps. 91. 15), or that encourage you from inward peace to bear cheerfully outward burdens (John 16. 33), or satisfy you of God's tenderness and moderation in His dealings with you (Isa. 27. 8), or that you shall reap blessed fruits from them (Rom. 8. 28), or that make clear your interest in God and His love under your afflictions (2 Sam. 7. 14), O what ease and relief ensues and how light is your burden compared with what it was before!

The Word tells us that there is no better way to improve our estates than to lay them out with a cheerful liberality for God, and that our withholding our hands when God and duty calls to distribute will not be for our advantage (Prov. 11. 24, 25; 19. 17; Isa. 32. 8).

Consult Providence now, and you will find it in all respects according to the report of the Word. O how true is the Scripture testimony in this respect! There are many thousand witnesses now living that can set their seals to both parts of this proposition. What men save (as they count saving) with one hand, Providence scatters by another hand; and what they scatter abroad with a liberal hand and single eye for God is surely repaid to them or theirs. Never did any man lose by distributing for God. He that lends to the poor lends to the Lord, or as some expound that text, puts his money to interest to the Lord. Some have observed how Providence has doubled all they have laid out for God, in ways unexpected to them.

The Word assures us that the best expedient for a man to settle his own interest in the consciences and affections of men is to direct his ways so as to please the Lord (Prov. 16. 7), and does not Providence confirm it? This the three Jews found by experience (Dan. 3. 28, 29) and so did Daniel (6. 20–22). This kept up John's reputation in the conscience of Herod (Mark 6. 20). So it proved when Constantius made that exploratory decree; those that were conscientious were preferred, and those that changed their religion expelled. Never did any man lose at last by his fidelity.

The written Word tells us that the best way to gain inward peace and tranquillity of mind under puzzling and disturbing troubles is to commit ourselves and our case to the Lord (Ps. 37. 5–7; Prov. 16. 3).

As you have read in the Word, so you have found it in your own experience. O what a burden is off your shoulders when you have resigned the case to God! Then Providence concludes your affairs comfortably for you. The difficulty is soon over when the heart is brought to this.

Thus you see how Scriptures are fulfilled by Providence in these few instances I have given. Compare them in all other cases and you will find the same, for all the lines of Providence lead from the Scripture, and return there again, and do most visibly begin and end there.

In all your reviews and observations of Providence, be sure that you eye God as the author or orderer of them all (Prov. 3. 6).

In all the comfortable providences of your lives, eye God as the author or donor of them. Remember He is 'the Father of mercies' that begets every mercy for you, 'The God of all comfort' (2 Cor. 1. 3) without whose order no mercy or comfort can come to your hands. And do not think it enough thus to acknowledge Him in a general way, but when you receive mercies, take special notice of the following particulars:

Eye the care of God for you. 'He careth for you' (1 Pet. 5. 7). 'Your heavenly Father knoweth that ye have need of these things' (Matt. 6. 32). You have but to acquaint Him what you need, and your needs are supplied. Be careful about nothing. (Phil. 4. 6); do not torture yourselves about it, you have a Father that cares for you.

Eye the wisdom of God in the way of dispensing His mercies to you, how suitably they are ordered to your condition, and how seasonably. When one comfort is cut off and removed, another is raised up in its room. Thus Isaac was comforted in Rebecca after his mother's death (Gen. 24. 67).

Eye the free grace of God in them, yea, see riches of grace in every bequest of comfort to so vile and unworthy creatures as you are. See yourselves surpassed by the least of all your mercies: 'I am not worthy of the least,' said Jacob (Gen. 32. 10).

Eye the condescension of God to your requests for those mercies (Ps. 34. 6). This is the sweetest bit in any enjoyment, in which a man can consciously relish the return and answer of his prayers, and it greatly inflames the soul's love to God (Ps. 116. 1).

Eye the design and end of God in all your comforts. Know that it is not sent to satisfy the cravings of your sensual appetite, but to quicken and enable you for a more cheerful discharge of your duty (Deut. 28. 47).

Eye the way and method in which your mercies are conveyed to you. They all flow to you through the blood of Christ and the covenant of grace (1 Cor. 3. 22, 23). Mercies derive their sweetness from the channel through which they run to us.

Eye the distinguishing goodness of God in all the comfortable enjoyments of your lives. How many thousands better than you are denied these comforts (Heb. 11. 37)!

Eye them all as comforts appointed to refresh you in your way to far better and greater mercies than themselves. The best mercies are still reserved till last, and all these are introductive to better.

In all the sad and afflictive providences that befall you, eye God as the author and orderer of them also. So He represents Himself to us: 'Behold, I create evil, and devise a device against you' (Jer. 18. 11). 'Is there evil in the city, and the Lord hath not done it?' (Amos 3. 6).

Set before you the sovereignty of God. Eye Him as a Being infinitely superior to you, at whose pleasure you and all you have subsist (Ps. 115. 3), which is the most conclusive reason and argument for submission (Ps. 46. 10). For if we, and all we have proceeded from His will, how right it is that we be resigned up to it! It is not many years ago since we were not, and when it pleased Him to bring us upon the stage of action, we had no liberty of contracting with Him on what terms we would come into the world, or refuse to be, except we might have our being on such terms as we desired. His sovereignty is gloriously displayed in His eternal decrees and temporal providences. He might have put you into what rank of creatures He pleased. He might have made you the most despicable creatures, worms or toads: or, if men, the most vile, abject and miserable among men; and when you had run through all the miseries of this life, have damned you to eternity, made you miserable for ever, and all this without any wrong to you. And shall not this quieten us under the common afflictions of this life?

Set the grace and goodness of God before you in all afflictive providences. O see Him passing by you in the cloudy and dark day, proclaiming His name, 'The Lord, The Lord God, merciful and gracious' (Ex. 34. 6). There are two sorts of mercies that are seldom eclipsed by the darkest affliction that befalls the saints in their temporal concerns, that is, sparing mercy in this world, and saving mercy in that to come. It is not so bad now as it might be, and we deserved it should be, and it will be better hereafter. This the Church observed, and reasoned herself quiet from it (Lam. 3. 22). Has He taken some? He might have taken all. Are we afflicted? It is a mercy we are not destroyed. O if we consider what temporal mercies are yet spared, and what spiritual mercies are bestowed and still continued to us, we shall find cause to admire mercy rather than complain of severity.

Eye the wisdom of God in all your afflictions. Behold it in the choice of the kind of your affliction, this, and not another; the time, now and not at another season; the degree, in this measure only, and not in a greater; the supports offered you under it, not left altogether helpless; the issue to which it is overruled, it is to your good, not ruin. Look upon these and then ask your heart that question God asked Jonah, 'Doest thou well to be angry?' (4. 9). Surely, when you consider all – what need you had of these rods, that your corruptions will require all this, it may be much more, to mortify them; that without the perishing of these things you might have perished for ever – you will see great reason to be quiet and well satisfied under the hand of God.

Set the faithfulness of the Lord before you under the saddest providences. So did David (Ps. 119. 75). This is according to His covenant faithfulness (Ps. 89. 32). Hence it is that the Lord will not withhold a rod when need requires it (1 Pet. 1. 6). Nor will He forsake His people under the rod when He inflicts it (2 Cor. 4. 9).

O what quietness will this breed! I see my God will not lose my heart, if a rod can prevent it. He would rather hear me groan here than howl hereafter. His love is judicious, not fond. He consults my good rather than my ease.

Eye the all-sufficiency of God in the day of affliction. See enough in Him still, whatever is gone. Here is the fountain still as full as ever, though this or that pipe is cut off, which was wont to convey somewhat of it to me. O Christians, cannot you make up any loss this way? Cannot you see more in God than in any or all the creature-comforts you have lost? With what eyes then do you look upon God?

Lastly, eye the immutability of God. Look on Him as the

Rock of ages, 'The Father of lights, with whom is no variableness, neither shadow of turning' (James 1. 17). Eye Jesus Christ as 'the same yesterday, to-day and for ever.' O how quietly will you then behave yourselves under the changes of providence! It may be, two or three days have made a sad change in your condition. The death of a dear relation has turned all things upside down; that place is empty where lately he was, as it is: 'neither shall his place know him any more' (Job 7. 10). Well, God is what He was, and where He was; time shall make no change upon Him. 'The grass withereth, the flower fadeth; but the word of our God shall stand for ever' (Isa. 40. 6–8). O how composing are those views of God to our spirits under dark providences!

Lastly, work up your hearts to those frames, and exercise those affections which the particular providences of God that concern you call for (Eccles. 7. 14).

As there are various affections planted in your souls, so there are various graces planted in those affections, and various providences appointed to draw forth and exercise these graces.

When the providences of God are sad and afflictive, either upon the Church in general, or your families and persons in particular, then it is seasonable for you to exercise godly sorrow and humility of spirit. For in that day and by those providences, God calls to it (Isa. 22. 12; Micah 6. 9). Now, sensual pleasure and natural joy is out of season: 'Should we then make mirth?' (Ezek. 21. 10). If there is a filial spirit in us, we cannot be light and vain when our Father is angry. If there is any real sense of the evil of sin which provokes God's anger, we must be heavy-hearted when God is smiting for it. If there is any sense and compassion for the miseries that sin brings upon the world, it will make us say with David: 'I beheld the transgressors, and was grieved' (Ps. 119. 158). It is sad to consider the miseries that they pull down upon themselves in this world and that to come. If there is any care in us to prevent utter ruin, and stop God in the way of His anger, we know this is the means to do it (Amos 4. 12).

However sad and dismal the face of Providence is, yet still maintain spiritual joy and comfort in God under all. 'Although the fig tree shall not blossom, neither shall fruit be in the vines; the labour of the olive shall fail, and the fields shall yield no meat; the flock shall be cut off from the fold, and there shall be no herd in the stalls: yet I will rejoice in the Lord, I will joy in the God of my salvation' (Hab. 3. 17–18).

There are two sorts of comforts, natural and sensual, divine and spiritual. There is a time when it becomes Christians to exercise both (Esth. 9. 22). And there is a time when the former is to be suspended and laid by (Ps. 137. 2), but there is no season wherein spiritual joy and comfort in God is unseasonable (1 Thess. 5. 16; Phil. 4. 4). This spiritual joy or comfort is nothing else but the cheerfulness of our heart in God, and the sense of our interest in Him and in His promises. And it is sure that no providence can render this unseasonable to a Christian.

Let us suppose the most afflicted and calamitous state a Christian can be in, yet why should sad providences make him lay aside his comforts in God, when those are but for a moment, and these eternal (2 Cor. 4. 17)?

Why should we give up our joy in God on account of sad providences without, when at the very worst and lowest ebb the saints have infinitely more cause to rejoice than to be cast down? There is more in one of their mercies to comfort them than in all their troubles to deject them. All your losses are but as the loss of a farthing to a prince (Rom. 8. 18).

Why should they be sad, as long as their God is with them in all their troubles? As Christ said: 'Can the children of the bridechamber mourn, as long as the bridegroom is with them?' (Mat. 9. 15). So say I: Can the soul be sad while God is with it? O I think that one promise, 'I will be with him in trouble' (Ps. 91. 15) should bear you up under all burdens. Let them be cast down that have no God to turn to in trouble.

Why should we be sad as long as no outward dispensation of Providence, however sad, can be interpreted as a mark or sign of God's hatred or enmity. 'There is one event to the righteous and wicked' (Eccles. 9. 2, 3). Indeed, if it were a sign of the Lord's wrath against a man, it would justify our dejection; but this cannot be so. His heart is full of love while the face of Providence is full of frowns.

Why should we be cast down under sad providences while we have so great security that even by the hands of these providences God will do us good, and all these things shall turn to our salvation (Rom. 8. 28)? By these God is but killing your lusts, weaning your hearts from a vain world, preventing temptations and exciting your desires after heaven. This is all the hurt they shall do you, and shall that sadden us?

Why should we give up our joy in God, when the change of our condition is so near? It is but a little while, and sorrows shall flee away. You shall never suffer again : 'God will wipe away all tears' (Rev. 7. 17). Well then, you see there is no reason on account of Providence to give up your joy and comfort in God. But if you will maintain it under all providences, then be careful to make sure of your interest in, and title to God. Faith may be separated from comfort, but assurance cannot.

Mortify your inordinate affections to earthly things. This makes providences that deprive and cross us so heavy. Mortify your opinion and affection, and you will lighten your affliction. It is strong affection that makes strong affliction.

Dwell much upon the meditation of the Lord's near approach; and then all these things will seem but trifles to you. 'Let your moderation be known unto all men. The Lord is at hand' (Phil. 4. 5).

Exercise heavenly-mindedness, and keep your hearts upon things eternal under all the providences with which the Lord exercises you in this world. 'Noah walked with God' (Gen. 6. 9), yet met with as sad providences in his day as any man that ever lived since his time. But alas! we find most providences rather stops than steps in our walk with God. If we are under comfortable providences, how sensual, wanton and worldly do our hearts grow! And if sad providences befall us, how cast down or disturbed we are! And this comes to pass partly through the narrowness, but mostly through the deceitfulness of our spirits. Our hearts are narrow and know not how to manage two businesses of such different natures, as earthly and heavenly matters are, without detriment to one of them. But certainly such a frame of spirit is attainable that will enable us to keep on in an even and steady course with God, whatever befall us. Others have attained it, and why not we? Prosperous providences are for the most part a dangerous state to the soul. The moon never suffers an eclipse but at full; yet Jehoshaphat's grace suffered no eclipse from the fulness of his outward condition, who 'had riches and honour in abundance. And his heart was lifted up in the ways of the Lord' (2 Chron. 17. 5, 6). David's life was as full of cares, turmoils, and encumbrances as most men we read of; yet how spiritual the attitude of his heart was, that excellent Book of Psalms, which was mostly composed amidst those turmoils, will acquaint us. The apostles were cast into as great necessities and suffered as hard things as ever men did; yet how raised and heavenly their spirits were amidst all! And certainly, if it were not possible to maintain heavenly-mindedness in such a state and posture of affairs, God would never exercise any of His people with such providences. He would never give you so much of the world to lose your hearts in the love of it, or so little to distract you with the care of it. If therefore we were more deeply sanctified, and the tendencies of our hearts heavenward more ardent and vigorous, if we were more mortified to earthly things and could but keep our due distance from them, our outward conditions would not at this rate draw forth and exercise our inward corruptions, nor would we hazard the loss of so sweet an enjoyment as our fellowship with God for the sake of any concern our bodies have on earth.

Under all providences maintain a contented heart with what the Lord allots you. be it more or less of the things of this world. This grace must run parallel with all providences. Learn how to be full, and how to suffer want, and in every state to be content (Phil. 4. 11, 12).

In this duty all men are concerned at all times and in every state, not only the people of God, but even the unregenerate also. I will therefore address some considerations proper to both. And first to the unregenerate, to stop their mouths from complaining and charging God foolishly when providence crosses them. Let them seriously consider these four things:

First, that hell and eternal damnation are the portion of their cup, according to the tenor of law and Gospel threatenings. Whatsoever therefore is short of this is to be admired as the fruit of God's stupendous patience and forbearance toward them. Ah, poor souls! Do you not know that you are men and women condemned to wrath by the plain sentence of the Law (Mark 16. 16; John 3. 36; 2 Thess. 1. 6, 7)? And if so, surely there are other matters to exercise your thoughts, desires, fears and cares about than these. Alas! if you cannot bear a frown of Providence, a light cross in these things, how will you bear the everlasting burnings? A man that is to lose his head tomorrow is not very concerned about what bed he lies on or how his table is furnished the night before.

Consider, though you are condemned persons and have no promise to entitle you to any mercy, yet there are very many mercies in your possession at this day. Be your condition as afflictive as it will, is life nothing? especially considering where you must sink to when that thread is cut. Are the necessary supports of life nothing? Does not Providence minister to you these things, though you daily disoblige it and provoke God to send you to your own place? But above all, are the Gospel and precious means of salvation nothing, by which you yet are in a capacity of escaping the damnation of hell? O what would the damned say if they were but put into your condition once more! What! and yet fret against God because everything else does not suit your desires!

Consider, that if ever you are rescued out of that miserable condition you are in, such cross providences as these you complain of are the most probable means to do it. Alas! prosperity and success is not the way to save but to destroy you (Prov. 1. 32). You must be bound in fetters and held in cords of affliction if ever your ear is to be opened to instruction (Job 36. 8–10). Woe to you if you go on smoothly in the way in which you are and meet with no crosses.

Lastly, consider that all your troubles, under which you complain, are pulled down upon your heads by your own sins. You turn God's mercies into sin and then fret against God because He turns your sins into sorrow. Your ways and doings procure these things to you. Lay your hand therefore upon your mouth and say, 'Wherefore doth a living man complain, a man for the punishment of his sins?' (Lam. 3. 39).

But now I must turn to the Lord's people, who have least pretences of all men to be dissatisfied with any of God's providences and yet are but too frequently found in that attitude. And to them I shall offer the following considerations:

Consider your spiritual mercies and privileges with which the Lord Jesus has invested you, and complain at your providential lot if you can. One of these mercies alone has enough in it to sweeten all your troubles in this world. When the apostle considered them, his heart was overwhelmed with astonishment, so that he could not forbear in the midst of all his outward troubles to cry out, 'Blessed be the God and Father of our Lord Jesus Christ, who hath blessed us with all spiritual blessings (Eph. 1. 3). Oh, who that sees such an inheritance settled upon him in Christ, can ever open his mouth again to complain at his providential lot!

Consider your sins, and that will make you contented with your lot. Yea, consider two things in sin: what it deserves from God, and what it requires to mortify and purge it in you. It deserves from God eternal ruin. The merit of hell is in the least vain thought. Every sin forfeits all the mercies you have; and if so, rather wonder your mercies are so many, than that you have no more. Besides, you cannot doubt but your corruptions require all the crosses, wants and troubles that are upon you, and it may be a great deal more, to mortify and subdue them. Do you not find, after all the rods that have been upon you, a proud heart still, a vain and earthly heart still? O how many bitter potions are necessary to purge out this tough malignant disease!

Consider how near you are to the change of your condition. Have but a little patience, and all will be as well with you as your hearts can desire. It is no small comfort to the saints that this world is the worst place that they shall ever be in; things will get better every day with them. If the traveller has spent all his money, yet it does not much trouble him if he knows himself to be within a few miles of his own home. If there are no candles in the house, we do not much trouble over it if we are sure it is almost break of day; for then there will be no use for them. This is the case with us; 'for now is our salvation nearer than when we believed' (Rom. 13. 11).

I have done with the directive part of this discourse, but before I proceed farther, I judge it necessary to leave a few cautions, to prevent the abuse of Providence.

If Providence delays the performance of any mercy to you that you have long waited and prayed for, yet see that you do not despond, nor grow weary of waiting upon God for that reason.

It pleases the Lord often to try and exercise His people this way, and make them cry: 'How long, Lord, how long?' (Ps. 13. 1, 2).

These delays, both for spiritual and temporal reasons, are frequent, and when they befall us we are too apt to interpret them as denials, and fall into a sinful despondency of mind, though there is no cause at all for it (Ps. 31. 12; Lam. 3. 8, 44). It is not always that the returns of prayer are despatched to us in the same hour they are asked of God; yet sometimes it falls out so (Isa. 65. 24; Dan. 9. 23). But though the Lord means to perform for us the mercies we desire, yet He will ordinarily exercise our patience to wait for them, and that for these reasons:

One is that our time is not the proper season for us to receive our mercies in. Now the season of mercy is a very great circumstance that adds much to the value of it. God does not judge as we do; we are all in haste and will have it now (Num. 12. 13). 'For the Lord is a God of judgment: blessed are all they that wait for him' (Isa. 30. 18).

Another reason is that afflictive providences have not accomplished that design upon our hearts they were sent for when we are so earnest and impatient for a change of them; and till then the rod must not be taken off (Isa. 10. 12).

Again, the more prayers and searchings of heart come between our needs and supplies, our afflictions and reliefs, the sweeter are our reliefs and supplies thereby made to us. 'Lo, this is our God; we have waited for him, and he will save us: this is the Lord, we have waited for him, we will rejoice and be glad in his salvation' (Isa. 25. 9). This recompenses the delay, and pays us for all the expenses of our patience.

But though there are such weighty reasons for the stop and delay of refreshing comfortable providences, yet we cannot bear it, our hands hang down and we faint. 'I am weary of my crying: my throat is dried: mine eyes fail while I wait for my God' (Ps. 69. 3). For alas! we judge by sense and appearance, and do not consider that God's heart may be towards us while the hand of His providence seems to be against us. If things continue as they are, we think our prayers are lost and our hopes perished from the Lord. Much more when things grow worse and worse and our darkness and trouble increase, as usually they do just before the break of day and change of our condition, then we conclude God is angry with our prayers. See Gideon's reply (Judges 6. 13). This even staggered a Moses' faith (Exod. 5. 22, 23). O what groundless jealousies and suspicions of God are found at such times in the hearts of His own children (Job 9. 16, 17; Ps. 77. 7–9)!

But this is our great evil, and to prevent it in future trials, I will offer a few proper considerations in the case.

First, the delay of your mercies is really for your advantage. You read, 'and therefore will the Lord wait that he may be gracious' (Isa. 30. 18). What is that? Why, it is nothing else but the time of His preparation of mercies for you, and your hearts for mercy, that so you may have it with the greatest advantage of comfort. The foolish child would pluck the apple while it is green; but when it is ripe, it drops of its own accord and is more pleasant and wholesome.

Secondly, it is a greater mercy to have a heart willing to refer all to God and be at His disposal than to enjoy immediately the mercy we are most eager and impatient for. In that, God pleases you; in this, you please God. A mercy may be given you as the fruit of common Providence; but such an attitude of heart is the fruit of special grace. So much as the glorifying of God is better than the satisfaction and pleasure of the creature, so much is such a frame better than such a fruition.

Thirdly, expected mercies are never nearer than when the hearts and hopes of God's people are lowest. Thus in their deliverance out of Egypt and Babylon (Ezek. 37. 11). So we have found it in our own personal concerns: 'At evening time it shall be light' (Zech. 14. 7). When we look for increasing darkness, light arises.

Fourthly, our unfitness for mercies is the reason why they are delayed so long. We put the blocks into the way of mercies and then repine that they make no more haste to us. 'Behold, the Lord's hand is not shortened that it cannot save: neither his ear heavy that it cannot hear: but your iniquities have separated between you and your God, and your sins have hid his face from you, that he will not hear' (Isa. 59. 1, 2).

Fifthly, consider that the mercies you wait for are the fruits of pure grace. You do not deserve them, nor can claim them upon any title of desert; and therefore have reason to wait for them in a patient and thankful frame.

Lastly, consider how many millions of men as good as you by nature are cut off from all hope and expectation of mercy for ever, and there remains to them nothing but 'a fearful expectation of wrath.' This might have been your case; and therefore do not be of an impatient spirit under the expectations of mercy.

Do not pry too curiously into the secrets of Providence, nor allow your shallow reason arrogantly to judge and censure its designs.

There are hard texts in the works as well as in the Word of God. It becomes us modestly and humbly to reverence, but not to dogmatize too boldly and positively upon them. A man may easily get a strain by over-reaching. 'When I thought to know this,' said Asaph, 'it was too painful for me' (Ps. 73. 16). 'I thought to know this'—there was the arrogant attempt of reason, there he pried into the arcana of Providence—'but it was too wonderful for me,' it was 'useless labour,' as Calvin expounds it. He pried so far into that puzzling mystery of the afflictions of the righteous and prosperity of the wicked, till it begat envy towards them and despondency in himself (Ps. 73. 3, 13), and this was all he got by summoning Providence to the bar of reason. Holy Job was guilty of this evil, and frankly ashamed of it (Job 42. 3).

I know there is nothing in the Word or in the works of God that is repugnant to sound reason, but there are some things in both which are opposite to carnal reason, as well as above right reason; and therefore our reason never shows itself more unreasonable than in summoning those things to its bar which transcend its sphere and capacity. Many are the mischiefs which ensue upon this practice.

By this we are drawn into an unworthy suspicion and distrust of the faithfulness of God in the promises. Sarah laughed at the tidings of the son of promise, because reason contradicted and told her it was naturally impossible (Gen. 18. 13, 14).

Hence comes despondency of mind and faintness of heart under afflictive providences. Reason can discern no good fruits in them, nor deliverance from them, and so our hands hang down in a sinful discouragement, saying all these things are against us (1 Sam. 27. 1).

Hence flow temptations to deliver ourselves by indirect and sinful means (Isa. 30. 15, 16). When our own reason fills us with a distrust of Providence, it naturally prompts us to sinful expedients, and there leaves us entangled in the snares of our own making.

Beware therefore you do not lean too much to your own reasonings and understandings. Nothing is more plausible, nothing more dangerous.

10

THE ADVANTAGES OF MEDITATING
ON PROVIDENCE

═══

Having given direction for the due management of this great and important duty, what remains but that we now set our hearts to it, and make it the constant work of every day throughout our lives. O what peace, what pleasure, what stability, what holy courage and confidence would result from such an observation of Providence as has been recommended! But alas! we may say with reference to the voices of divine Providence, as it is written: 'For God speaketh once, yea, twice, yet man perceiveth it not' (Job 33. 14). Many a time Providence has spoken instruction in duty, conviction for iniquity, encouragement under despondency, but we do not regard it. How greatly are we all wanting in our duty and comfort by this neglect! It will be needful therefore to spread before you the loveliness and excellence of walking with God in a due and daily observation of His providences, that our souls may be fully engaged to it.

First, let me offer this as a moving argument to all gracious souls; that *by this means you may maintain sweet and conscious communion with God from day to day*. And what is there desirable in this world in comparison with that! 'For thou, Lord, hast made me glad through thy work: I will triumph in the works of thy hands' (Ps. 92. 4). Your hearts may be as sweetly refreshed by the works of God's hands as by the words of His mouth. Psalm 104 is all spent in the consideration of the works of Providence which so filled the Psalmist's heart that, by way of ejaculation, he expresses the effect of it: 'My meditation of him shall be sweet' (verse 34).

Communion with God, properly and strictly taken, consists in two things, viz., God's manifestation of Himself to the soul, and the soul's answerable returns to God. This is that κοινωνία (fellowship) we have here with God. Now God manifests Himself to His people by providences as well as ordinances; neither is there any grace in a sanctified soul hid from the gracious influences of His providential manifestations. Sometimes the Lord manifests His displeasure and anger against the sins of His people in correcting and rebuking providences. His rods have a chiding voice: 'Hear ye the rod, and who hath appointed it' (Micah 6. 9). This manifestation of God's anger kindly melts and thaws a gracious soul, and produces a double sweet effect upon it, namely, repentance for sins past, and due caution against future sins.

It thaws and melts the heart for sins committed. Thus David's heart was melted for his sin when the hand of God was heavy upon him in affliction (Ps. 32. 4, 5). Thus the captive Church, upon whom fell the saddest and most dismal providence that ever befell any of God's people in any age of the world, see how their hearts are broken for sin under this severe rebuke (Lam. 2. 17–19).

And then it produces caution against sin for the time to come. It is plain that the rebukes of Providence leave this effect upon gracious hearts (Ezra 9. 13, 14; Ps. 85. 8).

Sometimes God cheers and comforts the hearts of His people with smiling and reviving providences, both public and personal. There are times of lifting up as well as casting down by the hand of Providence. The scene changes, the aspects of Providence are very cheerful and encouraging, their winter seems to be over. They put off their garments of mourning, and then, ah, what sweet returns are made to heaven by gracious souls! Does God lift them up by prosperity? they also will lift up their God by praises (Ps. 18, title, and verses 1–3). So Moses and the people with him (Exod. 15) when God had delivered them from Pharaoh, how they exalt Him in a song of thanksgiving which, for the elegance and spirituality of it, is made an emblem of the doxologies given to God in glory by the saints (Rev. 15. 3).

On the whole, whatever effects our communion with God in any of His ordinances is wont to produce upon our hearts, the same we may observe to follow our conversing with Him in His providences.

It is usually found in the experience of all the saints that in whatever ordinance or duty they have any conscious communion with God, it naturally produces in their spirits a deep abasement and humiliation from the sense of divine condescension to such vile poor worms as we are. Thus Abraham, 'which am but dust and ashes' (Gen. 18. 27). The same effect follows our converse with God in His providences. Thus when God had in the way of His providence prospered Jacob, how does he lay himself at the feet of God, as a man overwhelmed with the sense of mercy! 'I am not worthy of the least of all the mercies, and of all the truth which thou hast shown they servant; for with my staff I passed over this Jordan, and now I am become two bands' (Gen. 32. 10). Thus also it was with David: 'Who am I, O Lord God, and what is my house, that thou hast brought me hitherto?' (2 Sam. 7. 18). And I doubt not but some of you have found the same frame of heart upon you that these holy men here expressed. Can you not remember when God lifted you up by providence, how you cast down yourselves before Him and have been viler in your own eyes than ever! Why, thus do all gracious hearts. What am I, that the Lord should do thus and thus for me! O that ever so great and holy a God should thus be concerned for so vile and sinful a worm!

Does communion with God in ordinances melt the heart into love to God (Cant. 2. 3–5)? Why, so does the observation of His providences also. Never did any man converse with God's works of providence aright, but found his heart at some times melted into love to the God of his mercies. When God had delivered David from the hand of Saul and all his enemies, he said, 'I will love thee, O Lord my strength' (Ps. 18. 1 compared with the title). Every man loves the mercies of God, but a saint loves the God of his mercies. The mercies of God, as they are the fuel of a wicked man's lusts, so they are fuel to maintain a good man's love to God; not that their love to God is grounded upon these external benefits. 'Not thine, but thee, O Lord,' is the motto of a gracious soul, yet these things serve to blow up the flame of love to God in their hearts, and they find it so.

Does communion with God set the keenest edge upon the soul against sin? You see it does, and you have a great instance of it in Moses, when he had been with God in the mount for forty days and had there enjoyed communion with Him. When he came down and saw the calf the people had made, see what a holy paroxysm of zeal and anger it cast his soul into (Exod. 32. 19, 20). Why, the same effect you may discern to follow the saints' converse with God in His providences. What was that which pierced the heart of David with such a deep sense of the evil of his sin, which is so abundantly manifested in Psalm 51 throughout? Why, if you look into the title, you shall find it was the effect of what Nathan had laid before him, and if you consult 2 Samuel 12. 7–10 you will find it was the goodness of God manifested to him in the several endearing providences of his life, which in this he had so evilly requited the Lord for. It was the realization of this that broke his heart to pieces. And I doubt not but some of us have sometimes found the like effects by comparing God's ways and our own together.

Does communion with the Lord enlarge the heart for obedience and service? Surely it is as oil to the wheels, that makes them run on freely and nimbly in their course. Thus when Isaiah had obtained a special manifestation of God, and the Lord asked: 'Whom shall I send?' he presents a ready soul for the employment, 'Here am I; send me' (Isa. 6. 8). Why, the very same effect follows sanctified providences, as you may see in Jehoshaphat (2 Chron. 17. 5, 6) and in David (Ps. 116. 12). O when a soul considers what God has done for him, he cannot choose but say, What shall I return? How shall I answer these engagements?

And thus you see what sweet communion a soul may have with God in the way of His providences. O that you would thus walk with Him! How much of heaven might be found on earth this way! And certainly it will never repent the Lord He has done you good, when His mercies produce such effects upon your hearts. He will say of every favour thus improved, it was well bestowed, and will rejoice over you to do you good for ever.

A great part of the pleasure and delight of the Christian life is made out of the observations of Providence. 'The works of the Lord are great, sought out of all them that have pleasure therein' (Ps. 111. 2). That is, the study of Providence is so sweet and pleasant that it invites and allures the soul to search and dive into it. How pleasant is it to a well-tempered soul to behold and observe.

Observe the sweet harmony and consent of divine attributes in the issues of Providence! They may seem sometimes to jar and clash, to part with each other, and go contrary ways; but they only seem so to do, for in the winding up, they always meet and embrace each other. 'Mercy and truth are met together: righteousness and peace have kissed each other' (Ps. 85. 10). This is spoken with an immediate reference to that signal providence of Israel's deliverance out of the Babylonish captivity, and the sweet effects thereof. The truth and righteousness of God in the promises did, as it were, kiss and embrace the mercy and peace that was contained in the performance of them, after they had seemed for seventy years to be at a great distance from each other. For it is an allusion to the usual demonstration of joy and gladness that two dear friends are wont to give and receive after a long absence and separation from each other; they no sooner meet, but they smile, embrace and kiss each other. Even thus it is here. The Hebrew word may be rendered 'have met us,' and that also is true; for whenever these blessed promises and performances meet and kiss each other, they are also joyfully embraced and kissed by believing souls. There is, I doubt not, an indirect reference in this Scripture to the Messiah also, and our re-demeption by Him. In Him it is that these divine attributes, which before seemed to clash and contradict one another in the business of our salvation, have a sweet agreement and accomplishment. Truth and righteousness do in Him meet with mercy and peace in a blessed agreement. What a lovely sight is this, and how pleasant to behold! O, if we would but stand upon our watch-tower (Hab. 2. 3) to take due observations of Providence, what rare prospects might we have! Luther under-stands it of the Word of God, as much as to say, I will look into the Word, and observe there how God accomplishes all things, and brings them to pass, and how His works are the fulfilling of His Word. Others, as Calvin, understand it of a man's own retired thoughts and meditations, in which a man carefully observes what purposes and designs God has upon the world in general, or upon himself in particular, and how the truth and righteousness of God in the Word work them-selves through all difficulties and impediments, and meet in the mercy, peace and happiness of the saints at last. Every believer, take it in which sense you will, has his watch-tower as well as Habakkuk; and give me leave to say, it is an angelic employment to stand up and behold the consent of God's attributes, the accomplishment of His ends and our own happi-ness in the works of Providence. For this is the very joy of the angels and saints in heaven, to see God's ends wrought out and His attributes glorified in the mercy and peace of the Church (Rev. 14. 1–3, 8).

And as it is a pleasant sight to see the harmony of God's attributes, so it is exceedingly pleasant to behold the resur-rection of our own prayers and hopes as from the dead. Why, this you may often see, if you will duly observe the works of Providence towards you. We hope and pray for such and such mercies to the Church, or to ourselves; but God delays the accomplishment of our hopes, suspends the answer of our prayers and seems to speak to us: 'For the vision is yet for an appointed time, but at the end it shall speak and not lie: though it tarry, wait for it: because it will surely come, it will not tarry' (Hab. 2. 3). But we have no patience to wait the time of the promise, our hopes languish and die in the interim; and we say with the despondent Church, 'My hope is perished from the Lord' (Lam. 3. 18). But how sweet and comfortable it is to see these prayers fulfilled after we have given up all expectation of them! May we not say of them that it is even 'life from the dead.' This was David's case (Ps. 31. 22); he gave up his hopes and prayers for lost, yet lived to see the comfortable and unexpected returns of them. And this was the case of Job (6. 11); he had given up all expectation of better days, and yet this man lived to see a resurrection of all his lost comforts with an advantage. Think how that change and unexpected turn of Providence affected his soul. It is with our hopes and prayers as with our alms: 'Cast thy bread on the waters: for thou shalt find it after many days' (Eccles. 11. 1). Or as it was with Jacob, who had given over all hopes of ever seeing his beloved Joseph again, but when a strange and unexpected Providence had restored that hopeless mercy to him again, O how ravishing and transporting it was! (Gen. 46. 29, 30).

What a transporting pleasure it is to behold great blessings and advantages to us wrought by Providence out of those very things that seemed to threaten our ruin or misery! And yet by duly observing the ways of Providence you may to your singular comfort find it so. Little did Joseph think his transportation into Egypt had been in order to his advancement there; yet he lived with joy to see it and with a thankful heart to acknowledge it (Gen. 45. 5). Wait and observe, and you shall assuredly find that promise (Rom. 8. 28) working out its way through all providences. How many times have you been made to say as David, 'It is good for me that I have been afflicted' (Ps. 119. 71). O what a difference we have seen between our afflictions at our first meeting with them, and our parting from them! We have entertained them with sighs and tears but parted from them with joy, blessing God for them, as the happy instruments of our good. Thus our fears and sorrows are turned into praises and songs of thanksgiving.

What unspeakable comfort it is for a poor soul, that sees nothing but sin and vileness in itself, at the same time to see what a high esteem and value the great God has for him! This may be discerned by a due attendance to Providence, for there a man sees goodness and mercy following him through all his days (Ps. 23. 6). Other men pursue good, and it flies from them, they can never overtake it; but goodness and mercy follow the people of God, and they cannot avoid or escape it. It gives them chase day by day, and finds them out even when they sometimes put themselves by sin out of the way of it. In all the providences that befall them goodness and mercy pursue them. O with what a melting heart do they sometimes reflect upon these things! 'And will not the goodness of God be discouraged from following me, notwithstanding all my vile affronts and abuses of it in former mercies? Lord, what am I, that mercy should thus pursue me, when vengeance and wrath pursue others as good by nature as I am?' It certainly argues the great esteem God has of a man, when He thus follows him with sanctified providences, whether comforts or crosses, for his good. And so much is plain, from 'What is man . . . that thou shouldest visit him every morning, and try him every moment!' (Job 7. 17, 18). Certainly, God's people are His treasure, and by this it appears that they are so, that He withdraws not his eye from them (Job 36. 7). I say not that God's favour and respect to a man may be concluded solely from His providences, but sanctified providences may very much make it clear to us; and when it does so, it cannot but be matter of exceeding great joy.

What is there in all this world that can give a soul such joy and comfort as to find himself by everything set on and furthered in his way to heaven! And yet this may be discerned by a careful attendance to the effects and issues of providences.

However contrary the winds and tides of Providence at any time seem to us, yet nothing is more certain than that they all conspire to hasten sanctified souls to God and fit them for glory.

St. Paul knew that both his bonds and the afflictions added to them should turn to, or, as the word $\alpha\pi o\beta\acute{\eta}\sigma\epsilon\tau\alpha\iota$ imports, finally issue in his salvation. Not that in themselves they serve to any such purpose; but as they are overruled and determined to such an end, 'through your prayer and the supply of the Spirit of Jesus Christ' (Phil. 1. 19). When prayer, the external, and the Spirit, the internal means are joined with them, then afflictions themselves become excellent means to promote salvation. And have we not with joy observed how those very things that sense and reason tell us are opposite to our happiness have been the most blessed instruments to promote it! How has God blessed crosses to mortify corruption, wants to kill our wantonness, disappointments to wean us from the world! O we little think how comfortable those things will be in the review, which are so burdensome to present sense!

I beseech you consider what an effectual means the due observation of Providence will be to overpower and suppress the natural atheism that is in your hearts.

There is a natural seed of atheism in the best hearts, and this is very much nourished by passing a rash and false judgment upon the works of Providence. When we see wicked ones prospering in the world, and godly men crushed and destroyed in the way of righteousness and integrity, it may tempt us to think there is no advantage by religion and all our self-denial and holiness to be little better than lost labour. Thus stood the case with good Asaph : 'Behold, these are the ungodly, who prosper in the world; they increase in riches' (Ps. 73. 12). And what does the flesh infer from this? Why, no less than the unprofitableness of the ways of holiness : 'Verily I have cleansed my heart in vain, and washed my hands in innocency' (verse 13). This irreligious inference carnal reason was ready to draw from the dispensations of outward prosperity to wicked men; but now if we would carefully observe either the signal retributions of Providence to many of them in this world or to all of them in the world to come, O what a full confirmation is this to our faith! 'The Lord is known by the judgments which he executeth' (Ps. 9. 16). Psalm 58 contains the characters of the most prodigious sinners, whose wickedness is aggravated by the deliberation with which it is committed (verse 2) by their habit and custom in it (verse 3) and by their incorrigibleness and persistence in it (verses 4, 5). And the Providence of God is there invited to destroy their power (verse 6), and that either by a gradual and unperceived consumption of them (verses 7, 8) or by a sudden and unexpected stroke (verse 9).

And what shall the effects of such providence be to the righteous? Why, it shall be matter of joy (verse 10) and great confirmation to their faith in God: 'Verily there is a God that judgeth in the earth' (verse 11).

And, on the contrary, how convincingly clear are those providences that demonstrate the being, wisdom, power, love and faithfulness of God in the supporting, preserving and delivering of the righteous in all their dangers, fears and difficulties! In these things the Lord shows Himself to His people (Ps. 94. 1). Yea, He shows Himself to spiritual eyes in the providences, as clearly as the sun manifests itself by its own beams of light. 'And his brightness was as the light; he had horns coming out of his hand; and there was the hiding of his power' (Hab. 3. 3, 4). It is spoken of the Lord's going forth for His people in their deliverance from their enemies. Then He had horns or rays and beams of power and mercy coming out of His hands. By His hands are meant His providential administrations and dispensations, and the horns that came out of them are nothing else but the glorious display of His attributes in those providences. How did God make Himself known to His people in that signal deliverance of them out of Egypt? (Exod. 6. 3). Then He was known to them by His name Jehovah in giving being by His providences to the mercies promised.

Thus when Christ shall give His people the last and greatest deliverance from Antichrist, He shall show Himself to His people 'in a vesture dipped in blood, and his name shall be called, The Word of God' (Rev. 19. 13). His name was the Word of God before; but then He was the Word revealing and manifesting the promises and truths of God; now accomplishing and fulfilling them. 'For that thy name is near, thy wondrous works declare' (Ps. 75. 1).

But more particularly, let us bring it home to our own experience. It may be we find ourselves sometimes assaulted with atheistical thoughts. We are tempted to think God has left all things below to the course and sway of nature, that our prayers do not reach Him (Lam. 3. 44), that He does not regard what evils befall us. But tell me, saints, have you not enough at hand to stop the mouths of all such temptations? O do but reflect upon your own experiences, and solemnly ask your own hearts the following questions:

Have you never seen the all-sufficient God in the provisions He has made for you and yours, throughout all the way that you have gone? Who was it that supplied to you whatever was needful in all your straits? Was it not the Lord? 'He hath given meat unto them that fear him; he will ever be mindful of his covenant' (Ps. 111. 5). O do but consider the constancy, seasonableness and at some times the extraordinariness of these provisions, and how they have been given in answer to prayer, and shut your eyes if you can against the convincing evidence of that great truth: 'He withdraweth not his eyes from the righteous' (Job 36. 7).

Have you not plainly discerned the care of God in your preservation from so many and great dangers as you have escaped and been carried through hitherto? How is it that you have survived so many mortal dangers, sicknesses, accidents, designs of enemies to ruin you? It is, I presume, beyond question with you that the very finger of God has been in these things, and that it is by His care alone you have been preserved. When God had so signally delivered David from a dangerous disease and the plots of enemies against him, 'By this,' he says, 'I know thou favourest me, because mine enemy doth not triumph over me' (Ps. 41. 11). He gathered from those gracious protections the care God had over him.

Have you not plainly discerned the hand of God in the returns and accomplishments of your prayers? Nothing can be more evident than this to men of observation. 'I sought the Lord, and he heard me, and delivered me from all my fears. They looked unto him and were lightened, and their faces were not ashamed. This poor man cried, and the Lord heard him, and saved him out of all his troubles' (Ps. 34. 4–6). Parallel to this runs the experience of thousands and ten thousands of Christians this day; they know they have the petitions they asked of Him. The mercy carries the very impress and stamp of the duty upon it, so that we can say, This is the mercy, the very mercy I have so often sought God about. O how satisfying and convincing are these things!

Have you not evidently discerned the Lord's hand in the guiding and directing of your paths to your unforeseen advantage? Things that you never planned for yourselves have been brought about beyond all your thoughts. Many such things are with God; and which of all the saints has not found that word, 'The way of man is not in himself' (Jer. 10. 23) verified by clear and undeniable experience? I presume, if you will but look over the mercies you possess this day, you will find three to one, it may be ten to one, thus wrought by the Lord for you. And how satisfying beyond all arguments in the world are these experiences, that there is a God to whom His people are exceedingly dear, a God that performs all things for them (Ps. 57. 2)!

Is it not fully convincing that there is a God who takes care of you, inasmuch as you have found in all the temptations and difficulties of your lives His promises still fulfilled and faithfully performed in all those conditions? I appeal to yourselves, whether you have not seen that promise made good: 'I will be with him in trouble' (Ps. 91. 15) and that, 'God is faithful, who will not suffer you to be tempted above that ye are able: but will with the temptation also make a way of escape, that ye may be able to bear it' (1 Cor. 10. 13). Have not these been as clearly made out by Providence before your eyes, as the sun at noon-day? What room then is left for atheistical suggestions in your breasts?

The remembering and recording of the performances of Providence will be a singular support to faith in future exigencies. This excellent use of it lies full in the very eye of the text. There never befell David in all his troubles a greater strait and distress than this; and doubtless his faith had staggered had not the consideration of former providences come in to its relief. From this topic faith argues, and that very strongly and conclusively. So did David's faith in many exigencies. When he was to encounter the champion of the Philistines, it was from former providences that he encouraged himself (1 Sam. 17. 37). And the apostle Paul improves his experiences to the same purpose (2 Cor. 1. 9, 10). Indeed the whole Scripture is full of it. What Christian does not understand the exceeding usefulness of those experiences he has had to relieve and enliven? But I shall not satisfy myself with the common assertion, than which nothing is more trite in the lips of professors, but will labour to show you wherein the great usefulness of our recorded experiences, for encouraging faith labouring under difficulties, consists. To this purpose, I shall desire the reader to ponder seriously these following particulars:

Consider how much advantage those things have upon our souls which we have already felt and tasted, beyond those which we never relished by any former experience? What is experience but the bringing down of the objects of faith to the adjudication and test of spiritual sense? Now when anything has been once tasted, felt and judged by a former experience, it is much more easily believed and received when it occurs again. It is much easier for faith to travel in a path that is well known to it, having formerly trod it, than to beat out a new one which it never trod, nor can see one step before it. Hence it is, though there is a difficulty in all the acts of faith, yet scarce in any like the first venture it makes upon Christ; and the reason lies here, because in the subsequent acts it has all its former experiences to aid and encourage it; but in the first venture it has none at all of its own, it takes a path which it never knew before.

To trust God without any trial or experience is a more noble act of faith; but to trust Him after we have often tried Him is known to be more easy. O it is no small advantage to a soul in a new plunge and distress to be able to say, This is not the first time I have been in these deeps and yet emerged out of them. Hence it was that Christ rubbed up His disciples' memories with what Providence had formerly wrought for them in a day of need. 'O ye of little faith, why reason ye among yourselves, because ye have brought no bread? Do ye not yet understand, neither remember?' (Matt. 16. 8–11). As much as to say, Were you never in any need of bread before now? Is this the first difficulty that ever your faith met with? No, no, you have been in straits, and experienced the power and care of God in supplying them before now; and therefore I cannot but call you men of 'little faith'; for a very ordinary and small measure of faith, assisted with so much experience as you have had, would enable you to trust God. There is as much difference between believing before and after experience as there is between swimming with bladders and our first venture into the deep waters without them.

What a singular encouragement to faith do former experiences yield it, by answering all the pleas and objections of unbelief drawn from the object of faith! Now there are two things that unbelief stumbles at in God: His power and His willingness to help.

Unbelief maintains the impossibility of relief in deep distresses. 'Can God furnish a table in the wilderness? . . . Can he give bread also? Can he provide flesh for his people?' (Ps. 78. 19, 20). O vile and unworthy thoughts of God which proceed from our measuring the immense and boundless power of God by our own line and measure! Because we do not see which way relief should come, we conclude none is to be expected. But all these reasonings of unbelief are vanquished by a serious reflection upon our own experiences. God has helped, therefore He can. 'His hand is not shortened' (Isa. 59. 1). He has as much power and ability as formerly.

Unbelief queries the will of God, and questions whether He will now be gracious, though He has been so formerly. But after so many experiences of His readiness to help, what room for doubting remains? Thus Paul reasoned from the experience of what He had done to what He could do (2 Cor. 1. 10), and so did David (1 Sam. 17. 36). Indeed, if a man had never experienced the goodness of God to him, it were not so heinous a sin to question His willingness to do him good; but what place is left after such frequent trials?

It gives great encouragement to faith to answer the objections of unbelief drawn from the subject. Now these objections are of two sorts also.

First, such as are drawn from our great unworthiness. How, says unbelief, can so sinful and vile a creature expect that ever God should do this or that for me? It is true, we find He did great things for Abraham, Isaac, Jacob, Moses, etc., but these were men of eminent holiness, men that obeyed God and denied themselves for Him, and lived more in a day to His glory than ever I did all my days!

Well, but what signifies all this to a soul that under all its felt vileness and unworthiness has tasted the goodness of God as well as they? As unworthy as I am, God has been good to me notwithstanding. His mercy appeared first to me when I was worse than I am now, both in condition and disposition; and therefore I will still expect the continuance of His goodness to me, though I do not deserve it. 'For if when we were enemies, we were reconciled to God by the death of his Son, much more being reconciled, we shall be saved by his life' (Rom. 5. 10).

Secondly, such as are drawn from the extremity of our present condition. If troubles or dangers grow to a height and we see nothing but ruin and misery in the eye of reason before us, now unbelief becomes importunate and troublesome to the soul. Now where are your prayers, your hopes, yea, where is now your God?

But all this is easily put by and avoided by consulting our experiences in former cases. This is not the first time I have been in these straits, nor the first time I have had the same doubts and despondencies; and yet God has carried me through all (Ps. 77. 7–9). This is what prevents a Christian from losing all his hopes in an hour of temptation. O how useful are these things to the people of God!

The remembrance of former providences will minister to your souls continual matter of praise and thanksgiving, which is the very employment of the angels in heaven, and the sweetest part of our lives on earth.

If God will prepare mercy and truth for David, he will prepare praises for his God, and that daily (Ps. 61. 7, 8). 'By thee have I been holden up from the womb; thou art he that took me out of my mother's bowels'; there mercies from the beginning are recognized. 'My praise shall be continually of thee' (Ps. 71. 6); there the natural result of those recognitions is expressed.

There are five things belonging to the praise of God, and all of them have relation to His providences exercised about us:

(i) A careful observation of the mercies we receive from Him (Isa. 41. 17–20). This is fundamental to all praise. God cannot be glorified for the mercies we never noted.

(ii) A faithful remembrance of the favours received. 'Bless the Lord, O my soul, and forget not all his benefits' (Ps. 103. 2). Hence the Lord brands the ingratitude of His people, 'They soon forgat his works' (Ps. 106. 13).

(iii) A due appreciation and valuation of every providence that does us good (1 Sam. 12. 24). That providence that fed them in the wilderness with manna was a most remarkable providence to them; but since they did not value it at its worth, God had not that praise for it which He expected (Num. 11. 6).

(iv) The stirring up of all the faculties and powers of the soul in the acknowledgment of these mercies to us. Thus David: 'Bless the Lord, O my soul; and all that is within me bless his holy name' (Ps. 103. 1). Soul-praise is the very soul of praise: this is the very fat and marrow of that thank-offering.

(v) A suitable recompense for the mercies received. This David was careful about (Ps. 116. 1). And the Lord taxes good Hezekiah for the neglect of it (2 Chron. 32. 24, 25). This consists in a full and hearty resignation to Him of all that we have received by providence from Him, and in our willingness actually to part with all for Him when He shall require it.

Thus you see how all the ingredients to praise have respect to providences. But more particularly I will show you that, as all the ingredients of praise have respect to providences, so all the motives and arguments obliging and engaging souls to praise are found therein also. To this end consider how the mercy and goodness of God is exhibited by Providence to excite our thankfulness.

The goodness and mercy of God to His people is seen in His providences concerning them : and this is the very root of praise. It is not so much the possession that Providence gives us of such or such comforts as the goodness and kindness of God in the dispensing of them that engages a gracious soul to praise. 'Because thy lovingkindness is better than life, my lips shall praise thee' (Ps. 63. 3). To give, maintain and preserve our life are choice acts of Providence; but to do all this in a way of grace and lovingkindness, this is far better than the gifts themselves. Life is but the shadow of death without it. This is the mercy that crowns all other mercies (Ps. 103. 4). It is this a sanctified soul desires God would manifest in every providence concerning him (Ps. 17. 7), and what is our praising of God but our showing forth that lovingkindness which He shows to us in His providences? (Ps. 92. 1, 2).

As the lovingkindness of God manifested in Providence is a motive to praise, so the free and undeserved favours of God, dispensed by the hand of Providence, oblige the soul to praise. This was the consideration that melted David's heart into a thankful praising frame, even the consideration of the free and undeserved favours cast in upon him by Providence. 'Who am I, O Lord God, and what is my house, that thou hast brought me hitherto?' (2 Sam. 7. 18), that is, raised me by Providence from a mean condition to all this dignity; from following the ewes, to feed Jacob His people (Ps. 78. 70, 71). O this is what engages thankfulness (Gen. 32. 10)!

As the freeness of mercies dispensed by Providence engages praise; so the multitudes of mercies heaped this way upon us strongly oblige the soul to thankfulness. Thus David comes before the Lord encompassed with a multitude of mercies to praise Him (Ps. 5. 7). We have our loads of mercies, and that every day (Ps. 68. 19). O what a rich heap will the mercies of one day make, being laid together!

As the multitudes of mercies dispensed by Providence oblige to praise, so the tenderness of God's mercy, manifested in His providence, leaves the soul under a strong obligation to thankfulness. We see what tender regard the Lord has of all our needs, difficulties and burdens. 'Like as a father pitieth his children, so the Lord pitieth them that fear him' (Ps. 103. 13). He is 'full of bowels' as that word πολύσπλαγχνος (James 5. 11) signifies. Yea, there are not only bowels of compassion in our God, but the tenderness of bowels, like those of a mother to her sucking child (Isa. 49. 15). He feels all our pains as if the apple of His eye were touched (Zech. 2. 8), and all this is shown to His people in the way of His providences with them (Ps. 111. 2–4). O who of all the children of God has not often found this in His providences? And who can see it, and not be filled with thankfulness? All these are so many bands clapped by Providence upon the soul to oblige it to a life of praise. Hence it is that the prayers of the saints are so full of thanksgivings upon these accounts. It is sweet to recount them to the Lord in prayer, to lie at His feet in a holy astonishment at His gracious condescension to poor worms.

The due observation of Providence will endear Jesus Christ every day more and more to your souls. Christ is the channel of grace and mercy. Through Him are all the streams of mercy that flow from God to us, and all the returns of praise from us to God (1 Cor. 3. 21, 22). All things are ours upon no other title but our being His.

Now there are various things in Providence which exceedingly endear the Lord Jesus Christ to His people, and these are the most sweet and delightful parts of all our enjoyments.

The purchase of all those mercies which Providence conveys to us, is by His own blood; for not only spiritual and eternal mercies but even all our temporal ones are the acquisition of His blood. As sin forfeited all, so Christ restored all these mercies again to us by His death. Sin had so shut up the womb of mercy that had not Christ made an atonement by death it could never have brought forth one mercy to all eternity for us. It is with Him that God freely gives us all things (Rom. 8. 32): heaven itself, and all things needful to bring us thither, among which is principally included the tutelage and aid of divine Providence. So that whatever good we receive from the hand of Providence, we must put it upon the score of Christ's blood; and when we receive it, we may say, it is the price of blood; it is a mercy rising up out of the death of Christ; it cost Him dear though it come to me freely; it is sweet in the possession but costly in the acquisition. Now this is a most endearing consideration. Did Christ die that these mercies might live? Did He pay His invaluable blood to purchase these comforts that I possess? O what transcendent, matchless love was the love of Christ! You have known parents that have laid out all their stock of money to purchase estates for their children; but when did you hear of any that spent the whole stock and treasure of their blood to make a purchase for them? If the life of Christ had not been so painful and sad to Him, ours could not have been so sweet and comfortable to us. It is through His poverty we are enriched (2 Cor. 8. 9). These sweet mercies that are born of Providence every day are the fruits of 'the travail of his soul' (Isa. 53. 11).

The sanctification of all those mercies which Providence conveys to us is by our union with Christ. It is by virtue of our union with His person that we enjoy the sanctified gifts and blessings of Providence. All these are mercies additional to that great mercy, Christ (Matt. 6. 33). They are given with Him (Rom. 8. 32). This is the tenure by which we hold them (1 Cor. 3. 21–23). What we lost in Adam is restored again with advantage in Christ. Immediately upon the fall, that curse (Gen. 2. 17) seized upon all the miserable posterity of Adam and upon all their comforts, outward as well as inward; and this still lies heavy upon them. All that Providence does for them that are Christless is but to feed so many poor condemned wretches till the sentence they are under is executed upon them. It is indeed bountiful and openhanded to many of them and fills them with earthly comforts; but not one special sanctified mercy is to be found among all their enjoyments. These gifts of Providence do but deceive, defile and destroy them through their own corruptions, and for want of union with Christ. 'The prosperity of fools shall destroy them' (Prov. 1. 32). But when a man is once in Christ, then all providences are sanctified and sweet. 'Unto the pure, all things are pure' (Tit. 1. 15). 'A little that a righteous man hath is better than the treasures of many wicked' (Ps. 37. 16). Now Christ becomes a head of influence as well as of dominion; and in all things He consults the good of His own members (Eph. 1. 22).

The dispensation of all our comforts and mercies is by His direction and appointment. It is true, the angels are employed in the kingdom of Providence. They move the wheels, that is, are instrumental in all the revolutions in this lower world; but still they receive directions and orders from Christ, as you may see in that admirable scheme of providences (Ezek. 1. 25, 26). Now what an endearing meditation is this! Whatever creature is instrumental for any good to you, it is your Lord Jesus Christ that gave the orders and commands to that creature to do it; and without it they could have done nothing for you. It is your Head in heaven that consults your peace and comfort on earth; these are the fruits of His care for you. So in the prevention and restraints of evil; it is He that bridles the wrath of devils and men; He holds the reins in His own hands (Rev. 2. 10). It was the care of Christ over His poor sheep at Damascus that stopped the raging adversary who was upon the way, designing to destroy them (Acts 9).

The continuation of all your mercies and comforts, outward as well as inward, is the fruit of His intercession in heaven for you. As the offering up of the Lamb of God as a sacrifice for sin opened the door of mercy at first, so His appearing before God as a Lamb that had been slain still keeps that door of mercy open (Rev. 5. 6; Heb. 9. 24). By this His intercession our peace and comforts are prolonged to us (Zech. 1. 12, 13). Every sin we commit would put an end to the mercies we possess were it not for that plea which is put in for us by it. 'And if any man sin, we have an advocate with the Father, Jesus Christ the righteous : and he is the propitiation for our sins' (1 John 2. 1, 2). This stops all accusations, and procures new pardons for new sins. Hence it is 'he saves to the uttermost' (Heb. 7. 25), to the last completing act. New sins do not make void our former pardons nor cut off our privileges settled upon us in Christ.

The returns and answers of all your prayers and cries to heaven for the removing of your afflictions or supply of your needs are all procured and obtained for you by Jesus Christ. He is the master of your requests; and were it not that God had respect to Him, He would never regard your cries to Him nor return an answer of peace to you, however great your distresses might be (Rev. 8. 3, 4). It is His name that gives our prayers their acceptance (John 15. 16); because the Father can deny Him nothing, therefore your prayers are not denied. Does God condescend to hear you in the day of trouble? Does He convince you by your own experience that your prayers have power with God and do prevail? O see how much you owe to your dear Lord Jesus Christ for this high and glorious privilege!

The Covenant of Grace, in which all your comfortable enjoyments are comprised, and by which they are secured, sanctified and sweetened to you, is made in Christ and ratified by Him between God and you. Your mercies are all comprised in this covenant, even your daily bread (Ps. 111. 5), as well as your justification and other spiritual mercies. It is your covenant interest that secures to you whatever it comprises; hence they are called 'the sure mercies of David' (Isa. 55. 3). Nay, this is what sanctifies them and gives them the nature of special and peculiar mercies. One such mercy is worth a thousand common mercies. And being sanctified and special mercies, they must needs be exceedingly sweet beyond all other mercies. For these reasons it was that David so rejoiced in his covenant interest, though laden with many afflictions (2 Sam. 23. 5). But now all this hangs entirely upon Christ. The New Testament is in His blood (1 Cor. 11. 25), and whatever mercies you reap from that covenant, you must thank the Lord Jesus Christ for them. Put all this together, and then think how such considerations will endear Christ to your souls!

The due observations of Providence have a marvellous efficacy to melt the heart, and make it thaw and submit before the Lord.

How can a sanctified heart do less than melt into tears while it either considers the dealings of God from time to time with it, or compares the mercies received with the sins committed, or the different administrations of Providence towards itself and others!

Let a man but set himself to think deliberately and closely of the ways of Providence towards him, let him but follow the leading of Providence, as it has led him all along the way that he has gone, and if there is any principle of gracious tenderness in him, he shall meet with variety of occasions to excite and draw it forth.

Go back with your serious thoughts to the beginning of the ways of God with you, the mercies that broke out early in your youth, even the first-born mercies from the womb of Providence; and you will say, What need I go farther? Here is enough, not only to move, but overwhelm my heart. 'Wilt thou not from this time cry unto me, my Father, thou art the guide of my youth?'(Jer. 3. 4). What a critical time is the time of youth! It is the moulding age; and, ordinarily, according to

[164]

the course of those leading providences after-providences do steer their course. What levity, rashness, ignorance and strong propensities to sin and ruin accompanied that age! How many being then left to the sway of their own lusts run themselves into those sins and miseries which they never recover themselves from to their dying day! These, like the errors of the first concoction, are rarely rectified afterwards. Did the Lord guide you by His providence when but a child? Did He then preserve you from those follies and misdemeanours which blast the very blossom and nip the bud, so that no good fruit is to be expected afterwards? Did He then cast you into such families, or among such company and acquaintance, as moulded and formed your spirit into a better disposition? Did He then direct you into that way of employment in which you have seen so large a train of happy consequences ever since following you? And will you not from henceforth say: 'My Father, thou art the guide of my youth'?

Let us but bring our thoughts close to the providences of after-times, and consider how the several changes and removes of our lives have been ordered for us. Things we never foresaw nor designed, but much better for us than what we did design, have been all along ordered for us. The way of man is not in himself. God's thoughts have not been our thoughts, nor His ways our ways (Isa. 55. 8). Among the eminent mercies of your life, reader, how many of them have been mere surprises to you! Your own projects have been thrust aside to make way for better things designed by Providence for you.

Nay, do but observe the springs and autumns of Providence, in what order they have flourished and faded with you, and you will find yourself overpowered with the sense of divine wisdom and goodness. When necessity required, such a friend was stirred up to help you, such a place opened to receive you, such a relation raised up or continued to refresh you. And no sooner does Providence deprive you of any of them, but either your need of them ceases, or some other way is opened to you. O the depth of God's wisdom and goodness! O the matchless tenderness of God to His people!

Compare the dealings of Providence with you and others, yea, with others that sprang up with you in the same generation, it may be, in the same families and from the same parents, it may be in families greater and more flourishing in the world than yours, and see the difference, upon many great accounts, it has made between you and them. I knew a Christian who after many years' separation was visited by his own brother, the very sight of whom wrought upon him much as the sight of Benjamin did upon Joseph, so that he could not refrain to fall upon his neck and weep for joy; but after a few hours spent together, finding the spirit of his brother not only estranged from all that is spiritual and serious, but also very vain and profane, he hastened to his chamber, shut the door upon him, threw himself down at the feet of God and with flowing eyes and a melting heart admired the distinguishing grace of God, saying, 'Was not Esau Jacob's brother?' (Mal. 1. 2). O grace, grace, astonishing grace!

Compare the behaviour of Providence towards you, with your own behaviour towards the Lord; and it must needs melt your hearts to find so much mercy bestowed where so much sin has been committed. What place did you ever live in, where you cannot remember great provocations committed, and notwithstanding that, manifold mercies received? O with how many notwithstandings and neverthelesses has the Lord done you good in every place! What relationship has not been abused by sin, and yet both raised up and continued by Providence for your comfort! In every place God has left the marks of His goodness, and you the remembrances of your sinfulness. Give yourselves but leave to think of these things, and it will be strange if your hearts do not melt at the remembrance of them.

Or lastly, do but compare your dangers with your fears, and both with the strange outlets and doors of escape Providence has opened, and it cannot do less than overpower you with a full sense of divine care and goodness. There have been dark clouds seen to rise over you, judgment even at your door, sometimes threatening your life, sometimes your liberty, sometimes your estates, and sometimes your dearest relatives, in whom, it may be, your life was bound up. Remember in that day what faintness of spirit seized you, what charges of guilt stirring up fears of the issue within you. You turned to the Lord in that distress, and has He not made a way to escape, and delivered you from all your fears (Ps. 34. 4)?

O, is your life such a continued throng, such a mad hurry, that there is no time for Christians to sit alone and think on these things, and press these marvellous manifestations of God in His providences upon their own hearts? Surely, might these things but lie upon our hearts, talk with our thoughts by day and lodge with us at night, they would even force their passage down to our very reins.

Due observation of Providence will both beget and secure inward tranquillity in your minds, amidst the vicissitudes and revolutions of things in this unstable vain world.

'I will both lay me down in peace, and sleep; for thou, Lord, only makest me dwell in safety' (Ps. 4. 8). He resolves the sinful fear of events shall not rob him of his inward quiet, nor torture his thoughts with anxious forebodings. He will commit all his concerns into that faithful fatherly hand that had hitherto wrought all things for him, and he does not mean to lose the comfort of one night's rest, nor bring the evil of to-morrow upon today, but knowing in whose hand he was, wisely enjoys the sweet felicity of a resigned will.

Now this tranquillity of our minds is as much begotten and preserved by a due consideration of Providence as by anything whatever. Hence it was that our Lord Jesus Christ, when He would cure the disciples' anxious and distracting care about a livelihood, bids them consider the care Providence has over the birds of the air and the lilies of the field, how it feeds the one and clothes the other without any anxious care of theirs; and would have them well consider those providences, and reason themselves into a calm and sweet composure of spirit from those considerations (Matt. 6. 27–34).

Two things destroy the peace and tranquillity of our lives,

our bewailing past disappointments, or fearing future ones. But would we once learn prevision and provision to be divine prerogatives and take notice how often Providence baffles those that pretend to it, causing the good they foresaw, according to their conjectures, coming to their hand, yet to baulk them and flee from them: and the evil they thought themselves sufficiently secured from, to invade them; I say, would we consider how Providence daily baffles these pretensions of men, and asserts its own dominion, it would greatly conduce to the tranquillity of our lives.

This is a great truth, that there is no face of adversity so formidable, but being viewed from this station, would become amicable. Now there are several things in the consideration of Providence that naturally and kindly compose the mind of a Christian to peace, and bring it to a sweet rest, while events hang in a doubtful suspense.

First, the supremacy of Providence and its uncontrollable power in working. This is often seen in the good that it brings us in a way that is above the thoughts and cares of our minds, or labour of our hands. 'I had not thought,' said Jacob, 'to see thy face; and lo, God hath showed me also thy seed' (Gen. 48. 11). There is a frequent coincidence of providences in a way of surprise, which from no appearance or the remotest tendency of outward causes could be foreseen, but rather falls visibly contrary to the present scheme and state of our affairs. Nothing tends to convince us of the vanity and folly of our own anxieties and fears more than this does.

Second, the profound wisdom of Providence in all that it performs for the people of God. The wheels are full of eyes (Ezek. 1. 18), that is, there is an intelligent and wise Spirit that sits upon and governs the affairs of this world. This wisdom shines out to us in the unexpected, yea, contrary events of things. How often have we been courting some beautiful appearance that invited our senses, and with trembling shunned the formidable face of other things, when, notwithstanding, the issues of Providence have convinced us that our danger lay in what we courted and our good in what we so studiously declined! This also is a sweet principle of peace and quiet to the Christian's mind, that he knows not but his good may be intended in what seemed to threaten his ruin. Many were the distresses and straits of Israel in the wilderness, but all was to humble them, that he might do them good in the latter end (Deut. 8. 16). Sad and dismal was the face of that providence that sent them out of their own land into the land of the Chaldeans; yet even this was a project to do them good (Jer. 24. 5). How often have we retracted our rash and headlong censures of things upon experience of this truth, and been taught to bless our afflictions and disappointments in the name of the Lord! Many a time have we kissed those troubles at parting which we met with trembling. And what can promote peace under doubtful providences more effectually than this?

The experiences we have had throughout our lives of the faithfulness and constancy of Providence are of excellent use to allay and quieten our hearts in any trouble that befalls us. 'Hitherto hath the Lord helped us' (1 Sam. 7. 12). We never found Him wanting to us in any case hitherto. This is not the first strait we have been in nor the first time that our hearts and hopes have been low. Surely He is the same God now as heretofore, His hand is not shortened, neither does His faithfulness fail. O recount in how great extremities former experience has taught you not to despair!

The conjectures Christians may make of the way of Providence towards them from what its former methods have been towards them is exceedingly quieting and comfortable. It is usual with Christians to compare times with times and to guess at the issue of one providence by another. The saints know what course Providence usually holds and accordingly with great probability infer what they may expect from what in like cases they have formerly observed. Christian, examine your own heart and its former observations, and you will find, (as Ps. 89. 30–32) that it is usually the way of God to prepare some smart rods to correct you, when either your heart has secretly revolted from God and is grown vain, careless and sensual, or when your steps have declined and you have turned aside to commit iniquity. And then when those rods have been sanctified to humble, reduce and purge your heart, it is usually observed that those sad providences are then upon the change, and then the Lord changes the voice of His Providence towards you. 'Go and proclaim these words towards the north and say, Return thou backsliding Israel, saith the Lord; and I will not cause mine anger to fall upon you : for I am merciful, saith the Lord, and I will not keep anger for ever. Only acknowledge thine iniquity' (Jer. 3. 12, 13).

If therefore I find the blessed effects of the rod upon me, that it has done its work, to break the hard heart and pull down the proud heart and awaken the drowsy heart and quicken the slothful. negligent, lazy heart; now with great probability I may conjecture a more comfortable aspect of Providence will quickly appear, the refreshing and reviving time is nigh.

It is usual with Christians to argue themselves into fresh reviving hopes, when the state of things is most forlorn, by comparing the providences of God one with another.

It is a mighty composing meditation when we compare the providences of God towards the inanimate and irrational creatures with His providences towards us. Does He take care for the very fowls of the air for whom no man provides, as well as those at the door which we daily feed? Does He so clothe the very grass of the field, hear the young ravens when they cry for meat, and can it be supposed He should forget His own people, that are of much more value than these? (Matt. 6. 26, 30).

Or if we compare the bounty and care that Providence has expressed to the enemies of God, how it feeds and clothes and protects them, even while they are fighting against Him with His own mercies, it cannot but quieten and satisfy us, that surely He will not be wanting to that people upon whom He has set His love, to whom He has given His Son, and for whom He has designed heaven itself.

Lastly, it must needs quieten us, when we consider what the Lord did for us in the way of His providence, when we ourselves were in the state of nature and enmity against God. Did He not then look after us when we did not know Him, provide for us when we did not own Him in any of His mercies, bestow thousands of mercies upon us when we had no title to Christ or any one promise? And will He now do less for us since we are reconciled and become His children?

Surely, such considerations as these cannot but fill the soul with peace, and preserve the tranquillity of it under the most disturbing providences.

Due observations of the ways of God in His providences towards us have an excellent usefulness and aptitude to advance and improve holiness in our hearts and lives.

The holiness of God is manifested to us in all His works of providence. 'The Lord is righteous in all his ways, and holy in all his works' (Ps. 145. 17). The instruments used by Providence may be very sinful and wicked; they may aim at base ends and make use of wicked means to attain them; but it is certain God's designs are most pure and all His workings are so too. Though He permits, limits, orders and overrules many unholy persons and actions, yet in all He works like Himself; and His holiness is no more defiled and stained by their impurity than the sunbeams are by the noxious exhalations of a dunghill. 'He is the rock, his work is perfect; for all his ways are judgment; a God of truth, and without iniquity, just and right is he' (Deut. 32. 4). So that in all His providences He sets before us a perfect pattern of holiness, that we might be holy in all our ways, as our Father is in all His ways. But this is not all.

His providences, if duly observed, promote holiness by stopping up our way to sin. O if men would but note the designs of God in His preventive providences, how useful would it be to keep them upright and holy in their ways! For why is it that the Lord so often hedges up our way with thorns, as it is (Hos. 2. 6), but that we should not find out paths to sin? Why does He clog us but to prevent our straying from Him? 'And lest I should be exalted above measure through the abundance of the revelations, there was given to me a thorn in the flesh, the messenger of Satan to buffet me' (2 Cor. 12. 7). O it is good to attend to these works of God, and study the meaning of them. Sometimes Providence ruins a hopeful thriving project to better our condition, and frustrates all our labours and plans; why is this, but to hide pride from man? Should you prosper in the world, that prosperity might be your snare, and make you a proud, sensual, vain soul. The Lord Jesus sees this, and therefore withdraws the food and fuel from your corruptions. It may be you have a diseased, weak body, you labour under many infirmities. In this the wisdom and care of God over your soul is manifested; for were you not so clogged, how probable is it that much more guilt might be contracted! Your poverty does but clog your pride, reproaches clog your ambition, want prevents wantonness, sickness of body conduces to the prevention of many inward gripes of conscience, and groans under guilt.

The providences of God may be observed to conduce to our holiness, not only by preventing sin, that we may not fall into it; but also by purging our sins when we are fallen into them. 'By this therefore shall the iniquity of Jacob be purged; and this is all the fruit to take away his sin' (Isa. 27. 9). They are of the same use that fire and water are for purging and cleansing (Dan. 11. 33–35); not that they can purge us from sin in their own virtue and power, for if so, those that have most afflictions would have most grace also; but it is in the virtue of Christ's blood and God's blessing upon afflictive providences that they purge us from sin. A cross without a Christ never did any man good. Now in God's afflictive providences for sin there are many things that tend to the purging of it.

Such rebukes of Providence reveal the displeasure of God against us. The Lord frowns upon us in those providences. Our Father is angry, and these are the tokens of it; and nothing works more to the melting of a gracious heart than this. Must not the heart of a child melt and break while the father is angry? O this is more bitter to our spirits than all the smart and anguish of the affliction can be to our flesh. 'O Lord, rebuke me not in thy wrath; neither chasten me in thy hot displeasure: For thine arrows stick fast in me; and thine hand presseth me sore. There is no soundness in my flesh because of thine anger: neither is there any rest in my bones because of my sin' (Ps. 38. 1–3).

By these rebukes of sin the evil of sin is revealed more apparent to us, and we are made to see more clearly the evil of it in these glasses of affliction which Providence at such times sets before us, than we ever saw formerly. 'Thine own wickedness shall correct thee, and thy backslidings shall reprove thee: know therefore and see that it is an evil thing and bitter, that thou hast forsaken the Lord thy God, and that my fear is not in thee, saith the Lord God of hosts' (Jer. 2. 19). O the gall and wormwood that we taste in it under God's rebukes for it!

Providence blasts and frustrates all sinful projects to the people of God. Whoever else thrives in them, they shall not (Isa. 30. 1–5). And this also convinces them of the folly that is in sin, and makes them cleave to the way of simplicity and integrity.

Holiness is promoted in the soul by cautioning and warning the soul against sin for time to come. 'I have borne chastisement; I will not offend any more' (Job 34. 31). O happy providences, however smart, that make the soul for ever afraid of sin! Surely such rods are well bestowed. This gives God His end, and if ever we sorrowed after a godly sort, in the day of our troubles it will work this carefulness. 'For behold this selfsame thing, that ye sorrowed after a godly sort, what carefulness it wrought in you' (2 Cor. 7. 11). O if ever a man have been under a sanctified rod which has showed him the evil of sin and kindly humbled him for it; and a temptation should again solicit him to the same evil, why, thinks he, what a madness is it for me to buy repentance at so dear a rate? Have I not smarted enough already? You may as well ask me whether I will run again into the fire, after I have been already scorched in it.

To conclude – providences do greatly improve and promote holiness by drawing the soul into the presence of God, and giving it the opportunity and occasion of much communion with Him. Comfortable providences will do this; they will melt a man's heart in love to the God of his mercies and so pain his bowels that he shall not be quiet till he have found a place to pour out his soul in thankfulness to the Lord (2 Sam. 7. 18). Afflictive providences will drive us to the feet of God, and there make us to judge and condemn ourselves. And all this has an excellent use to destroy sin, and promote holiness in the soul.

Finally, the consideration and study of Providence will be of singular use to us in a dying hour. Hereby we treasure up that which will singularly sweeten our death to us, and greatly assist our faith in the last encounter. You find when Jacob died what reflections he had upon the dealings of God with him in the various providences of his life (Gen. 48. 3, 7, 15, 16). In like manner you find Joshua recording the providences of God when at the brink of the grave; they were the subject of his dying discourse (Josh. 24.). And I cannot but think it is a sweet close to the life of any Christian. It must needs sweeten a deathbed to recount there the several remarkable passages of God's care and love to us from our beginning to that day, to reflect upon the mercies that went along with us all the way, when we are come to the end of it. O Christians, treasure up these instances for such a time as that is, that you may go out of the world blessing God for 'all the goodness and truth' he has performed for you all your life long. Now the meditations of these things must needs be of great use in that day, if you consider the following particulars:

The time of death is the time when souls are usually most violently assaulted by Satan with horrid temptations and black suggestions. We may say of that figurative, as it is said of the natural serpent, 'he never exerts his utmost rage till the last encounter,' and then his great design is to persuade the saints that God does not love them, has no care nor regard for them nor their cries; though they pray for ease and cry for sparing mercy, they see none comes. He handles them with as much roughness and severity as other men; yea, many of the vilest and most dissolute wretches endure less torments, and are more gently handled than they. 'There are no bands in their death' (Ps. 73. 4), whereas you must go through a long lane of sickness to the grave and endure many deaths in one!

But what credit can these plausible tales of Satan obtain with a Christian who has been treasuring up all his life long the memorials of God's tender regard both to his needs and prayers, and who has carefully marked the evident returns of his prayers and gracious condescensions of God to him from his beginning to that moment? In this case his faith is mightily assisted by thousands of experiences which back and encourage it, and will not let the soul give up so easily a truth which he has so often felt and tasted. I am sure, says he, God has had a tender fatherly care of me ever since I became His. He never failed me yet in any former difficulty; and I cannot believe He will do so now. I know His love is like Himself, unchangeable. 'Having loved his own which were in the world, he loved them unto the end' (John 13. 1). 'For this God is our God for ever and ever, he will be our guide even unto death' (Ps. 48. 14). Did He love me in my youth, and will He cast me off in my decrepit age? 'O God,' said David, 'thou hast taught me from my youth; and hitherto have I declared thy wondrous works. Now also when I am old and gray-headed, O God, forsake me not' (Ps. 71. 17, 18).

At death the saints are engaged in the last and one of the most eminent works of faith, even the committing themselves into the hands of God when they are launching forth into that vast eternity and entering into that new state which will make so great a change to us in a moment. In this, Christ sets us a pattern: 'Father, into thy hands I commend my spirit; and having said thus he gave up the ghost' (Luke 23. 46). So Stephen at his death, 'Lord Jesus, receive my spirit' (Acts 7. 59), and immediately fell asleep.

There are two signal and remarkable acts of faith, both exceedingly difficult, viz., its first act and its last. The first is a great venture that it makes of itself upon Christ, and the last is a great venture too, to cast itself into the ocean of eternity upon the belief of a promise. But yet I know the first venture of the soul upon Christ is much more difficult than the last venture upon death; and that which makes it so is in great measure the manifold recorded experiences that the soul has been gathering up from the day of its espousals to Christ unto its dying, which is, in a sense, its marriage day. O with what encouragement may a soul throw himself into the arms of that God with whom he has so long conversed and walked in this world! whose visits have been sweet and frequent, with whom the soul has contracted so intimate acquaintance in this world; to whom it has committed all its affairs formerly and still found Him a faithful God; and now has no reason to doubt but it shall find Him so in this last distress and exigency also.

At death the people of God receive the last mercies that they shall ever receive in this world by the hand of Providence, and are immediately to make up their accounts with God for all the mercies that ever they received from His hand. What can be more suitable therefore to a dying person than to recount with himself the mercies of his whole life, the manifold receipts of favour for which he is to reckon with God speedily. And how shall this be done without a due and serious observation and recording of them now? I know there are thousands of mercies forgotten by the best of Christians; a memory of brass cannot contain them. And I know also that Jesus Christ must make up the account for us or it will never pass with God. Yet it is our duty to keep the accounts of our own mercies and how they have been used by us, for we are stewards, and then are to give an account of our stewardship.

At death we owe an account also to men, and stand obliged, if there is opportunity for it, to make known to them that survive us what we have seen and found of God in this world, that we may leave a testimony for God with men and bring up a good report upon His ways. Thus dying Jacob, when Joseph was come to take his last farewell of him in this world, strengthened himself and sat upon the bed and related to him the eminent appearances of God to him and the places where (Gen. 48. 2, 3), as also an account of his afflictions (verse 7).

So Joshua in his last speech to the people makes it his business to vindicate and demonstrate the truth of the promises by recounting to them how the Providence of God had fulfilled the same to a tittle in his day. 'And behold,' said he, 'this day I am going the way of all the earth: and ye know in all your hearts, and in all your souls, that not one thing hath failed of all the good things which the Lord your God spake concerning you; all are come to pass unto you, and not one thing hath failed thereof' (Josh. 23. 14).

And certainly it is of great importance to the world to understand the judgments and hear of the experiences of dying men. They of all men are presumed to be most wise and most serious. Besides, this is the last opportunity that ever we shall have in this world to speak for God. O then what a sweet thing would it be to close our lives with an honourable account of the ways of God! to go out of the world blessing Him for all the mercies and truth which He has here performed to us! How this would encourage weak Christians and convince the atheistical world that verily there is a reality and an excellence in the ways and people of God!

At death we begin the angelical life of praise and thanksgiving. We then enter upon that everlasting sweet employment; and as I doubt not but the providences in which we were concerned in this world will be a part of that song which we shall sing in heaven, so certainly it will become us to tune our hearts and tongue for it while we are here, and especially when we are ready to enter upon that blessed state. O therefore let it be your daily meditation and study what God has been to you and done for you from the beginning of His way hitherto.

And thus I have spread before you some encouragements to this blessed work. O that you would be persuaded to take up this lovely and in every way beneficial practice. This I dare presume to say, that whoever finds a careful and a thankful heart to record and treasure up the daily experiences of God's mercy to him shall never lack new mercies to record to his dying day. It was said of Claudian that he lacked matter suitable for the excellency of his powers; but where is the head or heart that is suitable for this matter? 'Who can utter the mighty acts of the Lord? who can show forth all his praise?' (Ps. 106. 2).

III

APPLICATION OF THE DOCTRINE OF PROVIDENCE

I I

PRACTICAL IMPLICATIONS FOR THE SAINTS

━━

If, as we have seen, God performs all things for you, God is to be owned by you in all that befalls you in this world, whether it is in a way of success and comfort, or of trouble and affliction. O it is your duty to observe His hand and disposal. When God gives you comforts, it is your great evil not to observe His hand in them. Hence was that charge against Israel: 'For she did not know that I gave her corn and wine and oil, and multiplied her silver and gold' (Hos. 2. 8); that is, she did not actually and affectionately consider my care over her and goodness to her in these mercies. And so for afflictions, it is a great wickedness when God's hand is lifted up not to see it (Isa. 26. 11). 'The ox knows his owner, and the ass his master's crib' (Isa. 1. 3); the most dull and stupid creatures know their benefactors. O look to the hand of God in all; and know that neither your comforts nor afflictions do arise out of the dust, or spring up out of the ground.

If God performs all things for you, how great is His condescension to and care over His people! 'What is man, that thou shouldest magnify him, and that thou shouldest set thine heart upon him? And that thou shouldest visit him every morning, and try him every moment?' (Job 7. 17, 18). Such is His tender care over you that He does not withdraw His eye from you (Job 36. 7). Lest any hurt you, He Himself will guard and keep you day and night (Isa. 27. 3). Should He withdraw His eye or hand one moment from you, that moment would be your ruin. Ten thousand evils watch but for such an opportunity to rush in upon you and destroy you and all your comforts. You are too dear to Him to be trusted in any hand but His own. 'All his saints are in thy hand' (Deut. 33. 3).

If God performs all things for you, see how obliged you are to perform all duties and services for God. It was the wish of a good man, 'O that I could be to God what my hand is to me,' viz., a serviceable useful instrument. Shall God do all things for you, and will you do nothing for God? Is Providence every moment at work for you, and will you be idle? To what purpose then is all that God has done for you? Is it not the aim and design of all, to make you a fruitful people? If God plant and fence and water you by Providence, surely He expects you to bring forth fruit (Isa. 5. 1–4). O that in return for all the benefits of Providence, you would say to God, as grateful Elisha said to the Shunammite, 'Behold, thou hast been careful for us with all this care. What is to be done for thee?' (2 Kings 4. 13), and with David, 'What shall I render unto the Lord for all his benefits towards me?' (Ps. 116. 12). He is ever doing you good; be you always abounding in His work. His providence stands by you in your greatest distresses and dangers; do not then flinch from God when His service and your duty is compassed about with difficulties. O be active for that God who every moment is active for you.

Does God perform all things for His people? Do not distrust Him then when new or great difficulties arise. Why should you think He that has done so many things for you will now do no more? Surely, 'the Lord's hand is not shortened that it cannot save; neither his ear heavy that it cannot hear' (Isa. 59. 1); if anything put a stop to His mercy, it is your iniquities, your distrust and infidelity. 'How long will it be ere you believe him?' If a thousand and ten thousand trials and experiences of His tender care, faithfulness and love will cure this unbelief in you, you have them at hand to do it. If the frequent confutations of this your distrust by the unexpected breakings-out of mercy for you under like discouragements will cure it, look back and you may see them. Certainly you have been often forced by Providence with shame and repentance to retract your rash censures of His care; and yet will you fall into the same unbelieving state again? O that you would once learn this great truth, that no man ever lacked that mercy which he did not lack a heart to trust and wait quietly upon God for. You never yet sought God in vain, except when you sought Him vainly.

Does God perform all things for you? Then seek God for all by prayer, and never undertake any design without Him.

Certainly, if He does not perform it for you, you can never have what you desire and labour for; and though He has designed to perform this or that mercy for you, yet for these things He will be enquired of, that He may do it for you (Ezek. 36. 37). I reckon that business as good as done, that mercy as good as if it were in hand, that trouble as good as over, for the doing, enjoying or removing of which we have engaged God by prayer. It is our folly to engage this instrument and that for us, to attempt this way and that to achieve our end, and all the while forget Him upon whose pleasure all instruments and means entirely depend. That which begins not with prayer seldom ends with comfort. 'The way of man is not in himself' (Jer. 10. 23); if it were, prayer might then be reckoned lost labour. O let Him that performs all be owned and acknowledged in all.

If God performs all things for us, then it is our great interest and concern in all things to study to please Him, upon whom we depend for all things.

It is a grave and weighty observation of Chrysostom that nothing should be grievous and bitter to a Christian but to provoke the displeasure of God. Avoid that, and no affliction or trouble whatever can cast down such a prudent soul; but even as a spark is easily extinguished in the sea, so will the favour of God extinguish those troubles. It is with such a soul, says he, as it is with the heavens; we think the heavens suffer when they are overspread with clouds, and the sun suffers when it is eclipsed; but there is no such thing, they do not suffer when they seem to suffer. Everything is well and shall be well, when all is well between us and God. The great consolation of the saints lies in this, that all that concerns them is in the hands of their Father. Luther said, 'I had utterly despaired had not Christ been head of the Church.' When He that performs all things is our God, even our God that delights in our prosperity, that rejoices over us to do us good, what ample security is here in the greatest confusions and dangers! When one told Borromeus that there were some that laid wait for his life, his answer was: 'What! is God in the world for nothing?' And as notable was the reply of Silentiarius in a like case: 'If God takes no care of me, how do I live? how have I subsisted hitherto?' Though it seems a romance to many, yet we must either quit the Scripture or give credit to this, that the most infallible rules for one to raise his fortune and ensure a destiny that can control the stars are given forth there, viz., in the Scriptures, where one can see *Sapiens dominabitur astris* (that he who knows the truth will govern the stars) and *quomodo unusquisque faber potest esse fortunae suae* (the means by which every man can shape his own fortune). A good man may even be his own carver. O that we would but steer our course according to those rare politics of the Bible, those divine maxims of wisdom! Fear nothing but sin. Study nothing so much as how to please God. Do not turn from your integrity under any temptation. Trust God in the way of your duty. These are sure rules to secure yourselves and your interest in all the vicissitudes of this life.

12

PRACTICAL PROBLEMS IN CONNECTION
WITH PROVIDENCE

———

*How may a Christian discover the will of God and his own
duty under dark and doubtful providences?*

In order to answer this question we must consider what is
meant by the will of God and what by those doubtful providences that make the discovery of His will difficult and what
rules are to be observed for ascertaining God's will for us
under such difficult and puzzling providences.

As to the will of God, it falls under a twofold consideration
of His secret and revealed will. This distinction is found in that
Scripture: 'The secret things belong unto the Lord our God:
but those things which are revealed belong unto us' (Deut.
29. 29). The first is the rule of His own actions; the latter of
ours, and this only is concerned in the query.

This revealed will of God is either manifested to us in His
Word or in His works. The former is His commanding will,
the latter His effecting or permitting will, the one concerning
good, the other evil. In these ways God manifests His will to
men, but yet with great variety and difference, both as to the
things revealed, the persons to whom He reveals them, and
the degrees of clearness in which they are revealed.

As to the things revealed, there is great difference. The great
and necessary duties of religion are revealed to us in the Word
with the greatest perspicuity and evidence; about these there
can be no hesitation. But things of a lower nature and lesser
concern are left more obscure.

As to the persons to whom God reveals His will, there is great difference. Some are strong men, others babes (1 Cor. 3. 1). Some have senses exercised, others are of weak and dull understanding; and we know everything is received according to the ability and measure of the person receiving it. Hence it is that one man's way is very plain before him, he knows what he ought to do; the other is ever and anon at a loss, dubious and uncertain what to do.

The manner of God's revealing His will to men is also very varied. Some have had special, personal and peculiar discoveries of it made to them. So had Samuel about the choice of the person whom he should anoint king (1 Sam. 9. 15). And so had David, for you find upon his enquiry of God, (probably by the Urim and Thummim), God told him what was his duty as to that expedition and what would be the event of it (1 Sam. 23. 2, 4, 9-12).

But now, all are tied up to the ordinary standing rule of the written word and must not expect any such extraordinary revelations from God. The way we now have to know the will of God concerning us in difficult cases is to search and study the Scriptures, and where we find no particular rule to guide us in this or that particular case, there we are to apply general rules and govern ourselves according to the analogy and proportion they bear towards each other.

Now it often falls out that in such doubtful cases we are entangled in our own thoughts, and put to a loss what course to take. We pray with David that God would make His way straight before us (Ps. 5. 8). Afraid we are of displeasing God and yet fearful we may do so, whether we resolve this way or that. And this comes to pass not only through the difficulty of the case but from our own ignorance and carelessness; and very frequently from those providences that lie before us, in which God seems to hint His mind to us, this way or that, and whether we may safely guide ourselves by those intimations of Providence is doubtful to us.

That God does give men secret hints and intimations of His will by His Providence cannot be doubted; but yet providences in themselves are no staple rule of duty nor sufficient discovery of the will of God. We may say of them: 'Behold, I go forward, but he is not there: and backward, but I cannot perceive him: on the left hand where he doth work, but I cannot behold him: he hideth himself on the right hand, that I cannot see him' (Job 23. 8, 9).

If Providence in itself is allowed to be a sufficient means of knowing God's will for us, then we shall often be forced to justify and condemn the same cause or person, forasmuch as there is one event happens to all, and as it falls out to the good, so to the wicked (Eccl. 9. 2). Besides, if Providence alone were the rule to judge any action or design by, then a wicked undertaking would cease to be so, if it should succeed well; but sin is sin still and duty is duty still whatever the events and issues.

The safest way therefore to make use of providences in such cases is to consider them as they follow the commands or promises of the Word and not singly and separately in themselves. If you search the Scriptures with an impartial and unbiassed spirit, in a doubtful case, pray for counsel and direction from the Lord, attend to the dictates of conscience. And when you have done all, you will find the providences of God falling out agreeably to the dictates of your own conscience and the best light you can find in the Word. You may in such cases make use of it as an encouragement to you in the way of your duty. But the most signal demonstrations of Providence are not to be accepted against a Scripture rule. No smiles or successes of Providence may in this encourage us to proceed; and on the other side, no frowns or discouragements of Providence should discourage us in the way of our duty, however many we should encounter therein. Holy Job could not find the meaning of God in His works, yet would he not go back from the commandments of His lips (Job. 23. 12). The like resolution you find in David to proceed in his duty and cleave to the Word, however many stumbling-blocks Providence should permit to be laid in his way. 'For I am become,' saith he, 'like a bottle in the smoke,' not only black, but withered up by troubles, 'yet do I not forget thy statutes' (Ps. 119. 83), and

'They had almost consumed me upon earth: but I forsook not thy precepts' (verse 87).

Paul, by the direction of the Spirit, was engaged to go to Jerusalem (Acts 20. 22). After a clear revelation of the mind of God to him in that matter, how many difficult and discouraging providences befell him in his way! The disciples at Tyre said to him 'through the Spirit,' though in that they followed their own spirits, 'that he should not go to Jerusalem' (Acts 21. 4).

Then at Caesarea he met Agabus, a prophet, who told him what should befall him when he came there (Acts 21. 10, 11), but all this will not dissuade him. And after all this, how passionately do the brethren beseech him to decline that journey (verses 12, 13)! Yet knowing his rule and resolving to be faithful to it, he puts by all and proceeds in his journey.

Well then, Providence in concurrence with the Word may give some encouragement to us in our way; but no testimony of Providence is to be accepted against the Word. If Scripture and conscience tell you such a way is sinful, you may not venture upon it, however many opportunities and encouragements Providence may permit to offer themselves to you, for they are only permitted for your trial, not your encouragement. Take this therefore for a sure rule, that no providence can legitimize or justify any moral evil. Nor will it be a plea before God for any man to say, The providence of God gave me encouragement to do it, though the Word gave me none. If therefore in doubtful cases you would discover God's will, govern yourselves in your search after it by the following rules:

(i) Get the true fear of God upon your hearts. Be really afraid of offending Him. God will not hide His mind from such a soul. 'The secret of the Lord is with them that fear him; and he will show them his covenant' (Ps. 25. 14).

(ii) Study the Word more, and the concerns and interests of the world less. The Word is a light to your feet (Ps. 119. 105), that is, it has a discovering and directing usefulness as to all duties to be done and dangers to be avoided. It is the great oracle at which you are to enquire. Treasure up its rules in your hearts, and you will walk safely. 'Thy Word have I hid in mine heart that I might not sin against thee' (Ps. 119. 11).

(iii) Reduce what you know into practice, and you shall know what is your duty to practice. 'If any man do his will he shall know of the doctrine' (John 7. 17). 'A good understanding have all they that do his commandments (Ps. 111. 10).

(iv) Pray for illumination and direction in the way that you should go. Beg the Lord to guide you in straits and that He would not permit you to fall into sin. This was the holy practice of Ezra : 'Then I proclaimed a fast there at the river Ahava, that we might afflict ourselves before our God, to seek of him a right way for us, and for our little ones, and for all our substance' (8. 21).

(v) And this being done, follow Providence so far as it agrees with the Word and no further. There is no use to be made of Providence against the Word, but in subservience to it. And there are two excellent uses of Providence in subservience to the Word. Providences, as they follow promises and prayer are evidences of God's faithfulness in their accomplishment. When David languished under a disease, and his enemies began to triumph in the hopes of his downfall, he prays that God would be merciful to him and raise him up (Ps. 41. 10); and by that, he says, he knew the Lord favoured him, because his enemy did not triumph over him (verse 11). This providence he looked upon as a token for good, as elsewhere he calls it (Ps. 86. 17). Also providences give us loud calls to those duties which the command lays upon us and tell us when we are actually and presently under the obligation of the commands as to the performance of them. Thus when sad providences befall the Church or ourselves, they call us to humiliation; and let us know that then the command upon us to humble ourselves at the feet of God is in force upon us. 'The Lord's voice crieth unto the city, and the man of wisdom shall see thy name. Hear ye the rod, and who hath appointed it' (Mic. 6. 9). The rod has a voice, and what does it speak? Why, now is the time to humble yourselves under the mighty hand of God. This is the day of trouble, in which God has bid you to call upon Him.

And on the contrary, when comfortable providences refresh us, it now informs us this is the time to rejoice in God, according to the rule: 'In the day of prosperity be joyful' (Eccl. 7. 14). These precepts bind always, but not to always. It is our duty therefore and our wisdom to distinguish seasons, and know the proper duties of every season; and Providence is an index that points them out to us. Thus far with the first case.

How may a Christian be supported in waiting upon God, while Providence delays the performance of the mercies to him for which he has long prayed and waited?

It is supposed in this case that Providence may linger and delay the performance of those mercies to us that we have long waited and prayed for, and that during that delay and suspense our hearts and hopes may be very low and ready to fail.

Providence truly may long delay the performance of those mercies we have prayed and waited upon God for. For the right understanding of this, know that there is a twofold term or season fixed for the performance of mercy to us: one by the Lord our God in whose hand are times and seasons (Acts 1. 7), another by ourselves who raise up our own expectations of mercies, sometimes merely through the eagerness of our desires after them and sometimes upon uncertain conjectural grounds and appearances of encouragement that lie before us.

Now nothing can be more precise, certain and punctual than is the performance of mercy at the time and season which God has appointed, however long it is, or however many obstacles lie in the way of it. There was a time prefixed by God Himself for the performance of that promise of Israel's deliverance out of Egypt; and it is said: 'And it came to pass at the end of the four hundred and thirty years, even the selfsame day it came to pass, that all the hosts of the Lord went out of the land of Egypt' (Exod. 12. 41). Compare this with Acts 7. 17, and there you have the ground and reason why their deliverance was not, nor could be delayed one day longer, because 'the time of the promise was now come.' Promises, like a pregnant woman, must accomplish their appointed months, and when they have so done, Providence will midwife the mercies they go big with into the world, and not one of them shall miscarry.

But for the seasons which are of our own fixing and appointment, as God is not tied to them, so His providences are not governed by them; and here are our disappointments, 'We looked for peace, but no good came; and for a time of health, and behold trouble' (Jer. 8. 15), and this is why we fret at the delays of Providence, and suspect the faithfulness of God in their performance, but His thoughts are not our thoughts (Isa. 55. 8). 'The Lord is not slack concerning his promise, as some men count slackness' (2 Pet. 3. 9). It is slackness if you reckon by your own rule and measure, but it is not so if you reckon and count by God's. The Lord does not compute and reckon His seasons of working by our arithmetic. You have both these rules compared, and the ground of our mistake detected in that Scripture: 'For the vision is yet for an appointed time, but at the end it shall speak, and not lie: though it tarry, wait for it: because it will surely come, it will not tarry' (Hab. 2. 3). God appoints the time; when that appointed time is come the expected mercies will not fail. But in the meantime, 'though it tarry,' says the prophet, 'wait for it, for it will not tarry.' Tarry, and not tarry, how shall this be reconciled? The meaning is, it may tarry much beyond your expectation, but not a moment beyond God's appointment.

During this delay of Providence the hearts and hopes of the people of God may be very low and much discouraged. This is too plain from what the Scriptures have recorded of others, and every one of us may find in our own experiences. We have an instance of this in Isaiah, where you have God's faithful promise that He will comfort His people, 'and will have mercy upon his afflicted' (49. 13). Enough, one would think, to raise and comfort their hearts. But the mercy promised was long in coming, they waited from year to year, and still the burden pressed them and was not removed. And therefore 'Zion said, the Lord hath forsaken me, and my Lord hath forgotten me' (verse 14); that is, it is in vain to look for such a mercy. God has no regard to us, we are out of His heart and mind; He neither cares for us nor minds what becomes of us.

So it was with David, after God had made him such a promise, and in due time so faithfully performed it, that never was mercy better secured to any man, for they are called, 'the sure mercies of David' (Isa. 55. 3), yet Providence delayed the accomplishment of them so long, and permitted such difficulties to intervene, that he despairs to see the accomplishment of them, but even concludes God had forgotten him too, 'How long wilt thou forget me, O Lord? for ever?' (Ps. 13. 1), and what he speaks here by way of question, he elsewhere turns into a positive conclusion: 'All men are liars' (Ps. 116. 11), 'I shall one day perish by the hand of Saul.' And the causes of these despondencies and sinkings of heart are partly from ourselves and partly from Satan.

If we duly examine our own hearts about it, we shall find that these sinkings of heart are the immediate effects of unbelief. We do not depend and rely upon the Word with that full trust and confidence that is due to the infallible Word of a faithful and unchangeable God. You may see the ground of this faintness in that Scripture: 'I had fainted unless I had believed' (Ps. 27. 13). Faith is the only cordial that relieves the heart against these faintings and despondencies. Where this is wanting, or is weak, no wonder our hearts sink at this rate, when discouragements are before us.

Our judging and measuring things by the rules of sense, this is a great cause of our discouragements. We conclude that according to the appearance of things will be their issues. If Abraham had done so, in that great trial of his faith, he had certainly lost his footing; but 'against hope', that is, against natural probability, he 'believed in hope, . . . giving glory to God' (Rom. 4. 18, 20). If Paul had done so, he had fainted under his trials. We faint not, said he, while we look not at the things that are seen (2 Cor. 4. 16, 18); as much as to say, that which keeps up our spirits is our looking off from things present and visible, and measuring all by another rule, viz., the power and fidelity of God firmly engaged in the promises.

In all these things Satan schemes against us. Hence he takes occasion to suggest hard thoughts of God, and to beat off our souls from all confidence in Him, and expectations from Him. He is the great mischief-maker between God and the saints. He reports and exploits the difficulties and fears that are in our way, and labours to weaken our hands and discourage our hearts in waiting upon God. And these suggestions gain the more credit with us, because they are confirmed and attested by sense and feeling.

But here is a desperate design carrying on under very plausible pretences against our souls. It concerns us to be watchful now, and maintain our faith and hope in God. Now blessed is he that can resign all to God, and quietly wait for His salvation. To assist the soul in this difficulty, I shall offer some further help in the following considerations:

Though Providence does not yet perform the mercies you wait for, yet you have no ground to entertain hard thoughts of God, for it is possible God never gave you any ground for your expectation of these things from Him.

It may be you have no promise to build your hope upon, and if so, why shall God be suspected and dishonoured by you in a case in which His truth and faithfulness was never engaged to you? If we are thwarted in our outward concerns, and see our expectations of prosperity dashed, if we see such and such an outward comfort removed, from which we promised ourselves much, why must God be blamed for this? These things you promised yourselves, but where did God promise you prosperity and the continuance of those comfortable things to you? Produce His promise, and show where He has broken it. It is not enough for you to say there are general promises in the Scripture, that God will withhold no good thing, and these are good things which Providence withholds from you; for that promise (Ps. 84. 11) has its limitations, it is expressly limited to such as 'walk uprightly.' It concerns you to examine whether you have done so, before you quarrel with Providence for non-performance of it. Ah, friend, search your own heart, reflect upon your own ways. Do you not see so many flaws in your integrity, so many turnings aside from God, both in heart and life, that may justify God, not only in withholding what you look for, but in removing all that you enjoy? And besides this limitation as to the object, it is limited (as all other promises relating to externals are) in the matter or things premised by the wisdom and will of God, which is the only rule by which they are measured out to men in this world, that is, such mercies in such proportions as He sees needful and most conducive to your good; and these given out in such times and seasons as are of His own appointment, not yours.

God never came under an absolute unlimited tie for outward comforts to any of us, and if we are disappointed, we can blame none but ourselves. Who bid us expect rest, ease, delight, and things of that kind in this world? He has never told us we shall be rich, healthy, and at ease in our habitations, but on the contrary, He has often told us we must expect troubles in the world (John 16. 33), and that we must 'through much tribulation enter into the kingdom of God' (Acts 14. 22). All that He stands bound to us by promise for is to be with us in trouble (Ps. 91. 15), to supply our real and absolute needs. 'When the poor and needy seek water, and there is none, and their tongue faileth for thirst, I the Lord will hear them, I the God of Israel will not forsake them' (Isa. 41. 17); and to sanctify all these providences to our good at last. 'And we know that all things work together for good to them that love God, to them who are the called according to his purpose' (Rom. 8. 28). And as to all these things, not one tittle ever did or shall fail.

If you say you have long waited upon God for spiritual mercies to your souls according to the promise, and still those mercies are deferred, and your eyes fail while you look for them, I would desire you seriously to consider of what kind those spiritual mercies are for which you have so long waited upon God.

Spiritual mercies are of two sorts: such as belong to the essence, the very being of the new creature, without which it must fail, or to its well-being and the comfort of the inner man, without which you cannot live so cheerfully as you would. The mercies of the former kind are absolutely necessary, and therefore put into absolute promises, as you see, 'And I will make an everlasting covenant with them, that I will not turn away from them to do them good; but I will put my fear in their hearts, that they shall not depart from me' (Jer. 32. 40). But for the rest they are dispensed to us in such measures and at such seasons as the Lord sees fit, and many of His own people live for a long time without them. The donation and continuation of the Spirit, to quicken, sanctify, and unite us with Christ, is necessary, but His joys and comforts are not so. A child of light may walk 'in darkness' (Isa. 50. 10). He lives by faith, and not by feeling.

You complain that Providence delays to perform to you the mercies you have prayed and waited for, but have you right ends in your desires after these mercies?

It may be that this is the cause you ask and receive not (James 4. 3). The lack of a good aim is the reason why we lack good success in our prayers. It may be we pray for prosperity, and our aim is to please the flesh. We look no higher than the pleasure and accommodation of the flesh. We beg and wait for deliverance from such a trouble and affliction, not that we might be the more ready and prepared for obedience, but freed of what is grievous to us and destroys our pleasure in the world. Certainly, if it is so, you have more need to judge and condemn yourselves, than to censure and suspect the care of God.

You wait for good, and it does not come; but is your will brought to a due submission to the will of God about it?

Certainly, God will have you come to this before you enjoy your desires. Enjoyment of your desires is the thing that will please you, but resignation of your wills is that which is pleasing to God. If your hearts cannot come to this, mercies cannot come to you. David was made to wait long for the mercy promised him, yea, and to be content without it before he enjoyed it. He was brought to be 'as a weaned child' (Ps. 131. 2), and so must you.

Your betters have waited long upon God for mercy, and why should not you?

David waited till his 'eyes failed' (Ps. 69. 3). The Church waited for Him in the way of His judgments (Isa. 26. 8). Are you better than all the saints that are gone before you? Is God more obliged to you than to all His people? They have quietly waited, and why should not you?

Will you lose anything by patient waiting upon God for mercies?

Certainly not! Yea, it will turn to a double advantage to you to continue in a quiet submissive waiting posture upon God. For though you do not yet enjoy the good you wait for, yet all this while you are exercising your grace; and it is more excellent to act grace than to enjoy comfort. All this time the Lord is training you up in the exercise of faith and patience, and bending your wills in submission to Himself, and what do you lose by that? Yea, and whenever the desired mercy comes, it will be so much the sweeter to you, for look how much faith and prayer has been employed to produce it, how many wrestlings you have had with God for it, so many more degrees of sweetness you will find in it when it comes. O therefore faint not, however long God delays you.

Are not those mercies you expect from God worth waiting for?

If not, it is your folly to be troubled for the lack of them. If they are, why do you not continue waiting? Is it not all that God expects from you for the mercies He bestows upon you, that you wait upon Him for them? You know you have not deserved the least of them at His hands. You expect them, not as a recompense, but as a free favour; and if so, then certainly the least you can do is to wait upon His pleasure for them.

Consider how many promises are made in the Word to waiting souls.

One Scripture declares, 'Blessed are all they that wait for him' (Ps. 30. 18). Another tells us that none that wait for him shall be ashamed (Ps. 25. 3), that is, they shall not be finally disappointed, but at last be made partakers of their hopes. A third Scripture tells us, 'They that wait upon the Lord shall renew their strength' (Isa. 40. 31), a promise you had need make much use of in such a fainting time, with many more of like nature; and shall we faint at this rate in the midst of so many cordials as are prepared to revive us in these promises?

How long has God waited for you to comply with His commands, to come up to your engagements and promises?

You have made God wait long for your reformation and obedience; and therefore you have no reason to think it much if God makes you wait long for your consolation. We have our 'how longs,' and has not God His? We cry: 'But thou, O Lord, how long?' (Ps. 6. 3). 'How long wilt thou forget me, O Lord? for ever? how long wilt thou hide thy face from me? How long shall I take counsel in my soul, having sorrow in my heart daily? how long shall mine enemy be exalted over me?' (Ps. 13. 1, 2). But surely we should not think these things long, when we consider how long the Lord has exercised His patience towards us. We have made Him say, How long, how long? Our unbelief has made Him cry, 'How long will it be ere they believe me?' (Numb. 14. 11). Our corrupt hearts have made Him cry, 'How long shall thy vain thoughts lodge within thee?' (Jer. 4. 14). Our impure natures and ways have made Him cry, 'How long will it be ere they attain to innocency?' (Hosea 8. 5). If God wait for you with so much patience for your duties, well may you wait upon Him for His mercies.

This impatience and infidelity of yours, expressed in your weariness to wait any longer, is a great evil in itself.

Very probably it is that evil which obstructs the way of your expected mercies. You might have your mercies sooner if your spirits were quieter and more submissive. And so much for the second case.

How may a Christian discern when a providence is sanctified, and comes from the love of God to him?

There are two sorts or kinds of providences which come to men in this world, the issues and events of which are vastly different, yea, contrary to each other.

To some all providences are overruled and ordered for good, according to that blessed promise (Rom. 8. 28); not only things that are good in themselves, as ordinances, graces, duties and mercies, but things that are evil in themselves, as temptations, afflictions, and even their sins and corruptions, shall turn in the issue to their advantage and benefit. For though sin is so intrinsically and formally evil in its own nature, that in itself it is not capable of sanctification, yet out of this worst of evils God can work good to His people. And though He never makes sin the instrument of good, yet His providence may make it the occasion of good to His people, so that spiritual benefits may, by the wise overruling of Providence, be occasioned by it.

And so for afflictions of all kinds, the greatest and sorest of them, under the influence of Providence bring a great deal of good to the saints, and that not only as the occasions, but as the instruments and means of it. 'By this therefore shall the iniquity of Jacob be purged' (Isa. 27. 9); that is, by the instrumentality of this sanctified affliction.

To others nothing is sanctified, either as an instrument or occasion of any spiritual good; but as the worst things are ordered to the benefit of the saints, so the best things wicked men enjoy do them no good. Their prayers are turned into sin (Ps. 109. 7), the ordinances are the savour of death (2 Cor. 2. 16), the grace of God turned into wantonness (Jude 4), Christ Himself a rock of offence (1 Pet. 2. 8), their table a snare (Ps. 69. 22), their prosperity their ruin (Prov. 1. 32). As persons are, so things work for good or evil. 'Unto the pure all things are pure; but unto them that are defiled and unbelieving is nothing pure' (Tit. 1. 15).

Seeing therefore the events of Providence fall out so opposite to each other upon the godly and ungodly, everything furthering the eternal good of the one, and the ruin of the other, it cannot but be acknowledged a most important case, in which every soul is deeply concerned, whether the providences under which he is, are sanctified to him or not?

For the understanding of this I shall premise two necessary considerations, and then give the rules which will be useful for the resolution of the question.

First, let it be considered that we cannot know from the matter of the things before us, whether they are sanctified or unsanctified to us; for 'no man knoweth either love or hatred by all the things that are before him; all things come alike to all' (Eccl. 9. 1, 2). We cannot understand the mind and heart of God by the things He dispenses with His hand. If prosperous providences befall us, we cannot say, This is a sure sign that God loves me, for who have more of those providences than the people of His wrath? 'They have more than heart could wish' (Ps. 73. 7). Surely that must be a weak evidence for heaven, which accompanies so great a part of the world to hell. By these things we may testify our love to God, but from ten thousand such enjoyments we cannot get any solid assurance of His love to us.

And from adverse afflictive providences we cannot know His hatred. If afflictions, great afflictions, many afflictions, long-continued afflictions, should set a brand or fix a character of God's hatred upon the persons on whom they fall, where then shall we find God's people in the world? We must then seek out the proud, vain, sensual wantons of the world, who spend their days in pleasure, and say these are the men whom God loves.

Outward things are promiscuously dispensed, and no man's spiritual state is discernible by the view of his temporal. When God draws the sword, it may 'cut off the righteous as well as the wicked' (Ezekiel 21. 3).

Secondly, though the providences of God materially considered afford no evidence of God's love to us, yet the manner in which they befall us, and the effects and fruits they produce in us, do distinguish them very manifestly; and by them we may discern whether they are sanctified providences and fruits of the love of God, or not. Yet these effects and fruits of providences by which we discern their nature do not always appear immediately; but time must be allowed for the soul's exercise under them. 'Now no chastening for the present seemeth to be joyous, but grievous: nevertheless afterwards it yieldeth the peaceable fruit of righteousness unto them which are exercised thereby' (Heb. 12. 11).

The benefit of a providence is discerned as that of a medicine is. For the present it gripes, and makes the stomach sick and loathing, but afterwards we find the benefit of it in our recovery of health and cheerfulness. Now the providences of God are some of them comfortable, and others sad and grievous to nature, and the way to discern the sanctification and blessing of them is by the manner in which they come, and their operations upon our spirits. I shall consider the case as it respects both sorts of providences, and show you what effects of our troubles or comforts will show them to be sanctified and blessed to us.

And first for sad and afflictive providences, in whatever kind or degree they befall us, we may warrantably conclude they are blessings to us, and come from the love of God, when they come in a proper season, when we have need of them, either to prevent some sin we are falling into, or recover us out of a remiss, supine, and careless frame of spirit into which we are already fallen. 'If need be, ye are in heaviness' (1 Pet. 1. 6). Certainly, it is a good sign that God designs your good by those troubles which are so fitted and wisely ordered to meet the need. If you see the husbandman pruning a tree in the proper season, it argues he aims at the fruitfulness and flourishing of it; but to do the same thing at midsummer speaks no regard to it, yea, his design to destroy it.

When our troubles are fitted both for quality and degree to work properly upon our most predominant corruptions, then they look like sanctified strokes. The wisdom of God is much seen in the choice of His rods. It is not any kind of trouble that will work upon and purge every sin; but when God chooses for us such afflictions as, like medicine, are suited to the disease the soul labours under, this speaks divine care and love. Thus we may observe that it is usual with God to smite us in those very comforts which stole away too much of the love and delight of our souls from God, and to cross us in those things from which we raised up too great expectations of comfort. These providences show the jealousy of God over us, and His care to prevent far worse evils by these sad but needful strokes. And so for the degrees of our troubles, sanctified strokes are ordinarily fitted by the wisdom of God to the strength and ability of our inherent grace. 'In measure, when it shooteth forth, thou wilt debate with it: he stayeth his rough wind in the day of the east wind' (Isa. 27. 8). It is an allusion to a physician, who exactly weighs and measures all the ingredients which he mingles in a potion for his sick patient, that it may be proportionate to his strength, and no more. And so much the next words intimate: 'By this therefore shall the iniquity of Jacob be purged' (verse 9).

It is a good sign that our troubles are sanctified to us when they turn our hearts against sin, and not against God. There are few great afflictions which befall men, but they make them quarrelsome and discontented. Wicked men quarrel with God, and are filled with discontent against Him. So the Scripture describes them: 'And men were scorched with great heat, and blasphemed the name of God, which hath power over these plagues' (Rev. 16. 9). But godly men, to whom afflictions are sanctified, they justify God and fall out with sin, they condemn themselves and give glory to God. 'O Lord, righteousness belongeth unto thee, but unto us confusion of faces' (Dan. 9. 7), and 'Wherefore doth a living man complain, a man for the punishment of his sins?' (Lam. 3. 39). Happy afflictions, which make the soul fall out and quarrel only with sin.

It is a sure sign that afflicting providences are sanctified when they purge the heart from sin, and leave both heart and life more pure, heavenly, mortified, and humble than they found them. Sanctified afflictions are cleansers, they pull down the pride, refine earthliness, and purge out the vanity of the spirit.

So you read (Dan. 11. 35) that it purifies and makes their souls white. Hence it is compared to a furnace which separates the dross from the pure metal: 'Behold I have refined thee but not with silver: I have chosen thee in the furnace of affliction' (Isa. 48. 10). But for wicked men, let them be never so long in the furnace, they lose no dross (Ezek. 24. 6). How many Christians can bear witness to this truth! After some sharp affliction has been upon them, how is the earthliness of their hearts purged! They see no beauty, taste no more relish in the world than in the white of an egg. O how serious, humble and heavenly are they, till the impressions made upon them by afflictions are worn off, and their deceitful lusts have again entangled them! And this is the reason why we are so often under the discipline of the rod. Let a Christian, says a late writer, be but two or three years without an affliction, and he is almost good for nothing. He cannot pray, nor meditate, nor discourse at that rate he was wont to do; but when a new affliction comes, now he can find his tongue, and come to his knees again, and live at another rate.

It is a good sign that afflictive providences are sanctified to us when we draw near to God under them and 'turn to him that smites us.' A wicked man under affliction 'revolts more and more' (Isa. 1. 5), 'turneth not unto him that smiteth him' (Isa. 9. 13), but grows worse than before; formality is turned into stupidity and indolence.

But if God afflicts His own people with a sanctified rod, it awakens them to a more earnest seeking of God, it makes them pray more frequently, spiritually, and fervently than ever. When Paul was buffeted by Satan he 'besought the Lord thrice' (2 Cor. 12. 8).

We may conclude our afflictions to be sanctified, and to come from the love of God to us, when they do not alienate our hearts from God, but inflame our love to Him. This is a sure rule: whatever ends in the increase of our love to God proceeds from the love of God to us. A wicked man finds his heart rising against God when He smites him, but a gracious heart cleaves the closer to Him; he can love as well as justify an afflicting God. 'All this is come upon us: yet have we not forgotten thee, neither have we dealt falsely in thy covenant. Our heart is not turned back, neither have our steps declined from thy way: though thou hast sore broken us in the place of dragons, and covered us with the shadow of death' (Ps. 44. 17–19). Here you have a true account of the attitude and frame of a gracious soul under the greatest afflictions. To be 'broken in the place of dragons, and covered with the shadow of death', imports the most dismal state of affliction; yet even then a gracious heart does not turn back, that is, does not for all this abate one drachm of love to God. God is as good and dear to him in afflictions as ever.

We may call our afflictions sanctified when divine teachings accompany them to our souls. 'Blessed is the man whom thou chastenest, O Lord, and teachest him out of thy law' (Ps. 94. 12). Sanctified afflictions are eye-salve; they teach us effectually, when the Spirit accompanies them, the evil of sin, the vanity of the creature, the necessity of securing things that cannot be shaken. Never does a Christian take a truer measure, both of his corruptions and graces, than under the rod. Now a man sees that filthiness that has been long contracting in prosperity, what interest the creature has in the heart, how little faith, patience, resignation and self-denial we can find when God calls us to the exercise of them. O it is a blessed sign that trouble is sanctified, when a man thus turns in upon his own heart, searches it, and humbles himself before the Lord for the evils of it!

In the next place, let us take into consideration the other branch of providences, which are comfortable and pleasant. Sometimes it smiles upon us in successes, prosperity, and the gratification of the desires of our hearts. Here the question will be how the sanctification of these providences may be known by us? For resolution in this matter, I shall for clearness sake lay down two sorts of rules: one negative, the other positive.

1. *Negative*. It is a sign that comfort is not sanctified to us, which does not come ordinarily in the way of prayer. 'For the

wicked boasteth of his heart's desire, and blesseth the covetous whom the Lord abhorreth. The wicked through the pride of his countenance will not seek after God; God is not in all his thoughts' (Ps. 10. 3, 4). Here you see Providence may give men 'their hearts' desire,' and yet they never once open their desires to God in prayer about it. But then those gifts of Providence are only such as are bestowed on the worst of men, and are not the fruits of love.

Whatever success, prosperity or comfort men acquire by sinful means and indirect courses are not sanctified mercies to them. This is not the method in which those mercies are bestowed. 'Better is a little with righteousness, than great revenues without right' (Prov. 16. 8), better upon this account that it comes in God's way and with His blessing, which never follows the way of sin. God has cursed the ways of sin, and no blessing can follow them.

Whatever prosperity and success makes men forget God and cast off the care of duty is not sanctified to them. It is unsanctified prosperity which lulls men asleep into a deep oblivion of God. 'He made him ride on the high places of the earth, that he might eat the increase of the fields; and he made him to suck honey out of the rock, and oil out of the flinty rock; butter of kine, and milk of sheep, with fat of lambs, and rams of the breed of Bashan, and goats, with the fat of kidneys of wheat; and thou didst drink the pure blood of the grape. But Jeshurun waxed fat, and kicked; thou art waxen fat, thou art grown thick, thou art covered with fatness; then he forsook God which made him, and lightly esteemed the Rock of his salvation' (Deut. 32. 13–15). 'Of the Rock that begat thee thou art unmindful, and hast forgotten God that formed thee' (verse 18). *Rarè fumant felicibus aræ* (There is little stench of sacrifice on the altars of the rich).

When prosperity is abused to sensuality and merely serves as fuel to maintain fleshly lusts, it is not sanctified. 'They send forth their little ones like a flock, and their children dance. They take the timbrel and harp, and rejoice at the sound of the organ. They spend their days in wealth, and in a moment go down to the grave' (Job 21. 11–13).

It is a sign that prosperity is not sanctified to men, when it swells the heart with pride and self-conceitedness. 'At the end of twelve months he walked in the palace of the kingdom of Babylon. The king spake and said, Is not this great Babylon that I have built for the house of the kingdom, by the might of my power and for the honour of my majesty?' (Dan. 4. 29–30).

That success is not sanctified to men which takes them from off their duty, and makes them wholly negligent or very much indisposed to it. 'O generation, see ye the Word of the Lord. Have I been a wilderness unto Israel, a land of darkness? Wherefore say my people, We are lords; we will come no more unto thee?' (Jer. 2. 31).

Nor can we think that prosperity sanctified, which wholly swallows up the souls of men in their own enjoyments, and makes them regardless of public miseries or sins. 'They lie upon beds of ivory, and stretch themselves upon their couches, and eat the lambs out of the flock, and the calves out of the midst of the stall; they chant to the sound of the viol, and invent to themselves instruments of music like David. They drink wine in bowls, and anoint themselves with the chief ointments; but they are not grieved for the afflictions of Joseph' (Amos 6. 4–6).

(ii) *Positive*. Those mercies and comforts are undoubtedly sanctified to men which humble their souls kindly before God in the sense of their own vileness and unworthiness of them. 'And Jacob said, . . . I am not worthy of the least of all thy mercies, and of all the truth which thou hast shown unto thy servant' (Gen. 32. 9, 10).

Sanctified mercies are commonly turned into cautions against sin (Ezra 9. 13). They are so many bands of restraint upon the soul that has them, to make them shun sin.

They will engage a man's heart in love to the God of His mercies (Ps. 18. 1, cf. title).

They never satisfy a man as his portion, nor will the soul

[205]

accept all the prosperity in the world upon that score. 'Esteeming the reproach of Christ greater riches than the treasures in Egypt: for he had respect unto the recompence of the reward' (Heb. 11. 26).

Nor do they make men regardless of public sins or miseries (Neh. 2. 1–3, compared with Acts 7. 23).

It is a sure sign that mercies are sanctified when they make the soul more ready and enlarged for God in duty. 'Therefore the Lord established the kingdom in his hand: and all Judah brought to Jehoshaphat presents, and he had riches and honour in abundance. And his heart was lifted up in the ways of the Lord' (2 Chron. 17. 5, 6).

That which is obtained by prayer and returned to God again in due praise, carries its own testimonials with it, that it came from the love of God, and is a sanctified mercy to the soul.

And so much for this third case.

How may we attain an evenness and steadiness of spirit under the changes and contrary aspects of Providence upon us?

Three things are supposed in this case: (i) that Providence has various and contrary aspects upon the people of God; (ii) that it is a common thing with them to experience great disorders of spirit under those changes of Providence; (iii) that these disorders may be, at least in a great measure, prevented by the due use and application of those rules and helps that God has given us in such cases.

That Providence has various, yea, contrary aspects upon the people of God, is a case so plain that it needs no more than the mentioning to commend it to all our understandings. Which of all the people of God have not felt this truth? Providence rings the changes all the world over. 'He increaseth the nations, and destroyeth them; he enlargeth the nations, and straiteneth them again' (Job 12. 23). The same it does with persons: 'Thou hast lifted me up, and cast me down' (Ps. 102. 10). See what a sad alteration Providence made upon the Church: 'How doth the city sit solitary that was full of people! how is she become as a widow! she that was great among the nations, and princess among the provinces, how is she become tributary!' (Lam. 1. 1). 'Is it nothing to you, all ye that pass by? behold, and see if there be any sorrow like unto my sorrow, which is done unto me, wherewith the Lord hath afflicted me in the day of his fierce anger' (verse 12). And how great an instance was Job of this truth? (Job 29 and 30 compared). How many thousands have complained with Naomi, whose condition has been so strangely altered, that others have said, as the people of Bethlehem did of her: 'Is this Naomi?' (Ruth 1. 19).

These vicissitudes of Providence commonly cause great disorders of spirit in the best men. As intense heat and cold try the strength and soundness of the constitution of our bodies, so the alterations made by Providence upon our conditions try the strength of our graces, and too often reveal the weakness and corruption of holy men. Hezekiah was a good man, but yet his weakness and corruption was betrayed by the alterations Providence made upon his conditions. When sickness and pains summoned him to the grave, what bitter complaints and despondencies are recorded (Isa. 38)! And when Providence lifted him up again into a prosperous condition, what ostentation and vain-glory did he show (Isa. 39. 2)! David had more than a common stock of inherent grace, yet not enough to keep him in an evenness of spirit under great alterations. 'And in my prosperity I said, I shall never be moved; thou didst hide thy face and I was troubled' (Ps. 30. 6, 7). It is not every man that can say with Paul, 'I know both how to be abased, and I know how to abound; everywhere and in all things I am instructed, both to be full and to be hungry, both to abound and to suffer need' (Phil. 4. 12). He is truly rich in grace whose riches or poverty neither hinders the acting nor impoverishes the stock of his graces.

Though the best men are subject to such disorders of heart under the changes of Providence, yet these disorders may in a great measure be prevented by the due application of such rules and helps as God has given us in such cases, and these shall be considered accordingly.

How may we attain to an evenness and steadiness of heart under the comfortable aspects of Providence upon us?

Under providences of this kind, the great danger is lest the heart be lifted up with pride and vanity, and fall into a drowsy and remiss condition. To prevent this, we had need urge humbling and awakening considerations upon our own hearts, such as the following:

These gifts of Providence are common to the worst of men, and are no special distinguishing fruits of God's love. The vilest of men have been filled even to satiety with these things. 'Their eyes stand out with fatness: they have more than heart could wish' (Psa. 73. 7).

Think how unstable and changeable all these things are. What you glory in to-day may be none of yours to-morrow. 'For riches certainly make themselves wings; they fly away as an eagle towards heaven' (Prov. 23. 5). As the wings of a fowl grow out of the substance of its body, so the cause of the creature's transitoriness is in itself. It is subjected to vanity, and that vanity, like wings, carries it away; they are but fading flowers (James 1. 10).

The change of providences is never nearer to the people of God than when their hearts are lifted up, or grown secure by prosperity. Does Hezekiah glory in his treasures? The next news he hears is of an impoverishing providence at hand (Isa. 39. 2–7). Others may be left to perish in unsanctified prosperity, but you shall not.

This is a great revelation of the carnality and corruption that is in your heart. It argues a heart little set upon God, little mortified to the world, little acquainted with the vanity and ensnaring nature of these things. O you do not know what hearts you have till such providences try them! And is not such a discovery matter of deep humiliation?

Was it not better with you in a low condition than it is now? Reflect, and compare state with state, and time with time. How is the frame of your hearts altered with the alteration of your condition? So God complains of Israel: 'I did know thee in the wilderness, in the land of great drought.

According to their pasture, so were they filled: they were filled, and their heart was exalted; therefore have they forgotten me' (Hosea 13. 5, 6); as much as to say, You and I were better acquainted formerly when you were in a low condition; prosperity has estranged you and altered the case. How sad it is that God's mercies should be the occasion of our estrangement from Him!

How may our hearts be established and kept steady under calamitous and adverse providences?

Here we are in equal danger of the other extreme, viz., despondency and sinking under the frowns and strokes of contrary providences. Now, to support and establish the heart in this case, consider the following:

Afflictive providences are of great use to the people of God; they cannot live without them. The earth does not need more chastening frosts and mellowing snows than our hearts do nipping providences. Let the best Christian be but a few years without them, and he will be aware of the need of them; he will find a sad remissness and declining upon all his graces.

No stroke of calamity upon the people of God can separate them from Christ. 'Who shall separate us from the love of Christ? Shall tribulation?' (Rom. 8. 35). There was a time when Job could call nothing in this world his own but trouble. He could not say, My estate, my honour, my health, my children, for all these were gone; yet then he could say: 'My Redeemer' (19. 25). Well then, there is no cause to sink while interest in Christ remains sure to us.

All your calamities will have an end shortly. The longest day of the saints' troubles has an end; and then no more troubles for ever. The troubles of the wicked will be to eternity, but you shall suffer but a while (1 Pet. 5. 10). If a thousand troubles are appointed for you, they will come to one at last, and after that no more. Yea, and though 'our light afflictions are but for a moment,' yet they work 'for us a far more exceeding and eternal weight of glory' (2 Cor. 4. 17). Let that support your hearts under all your sufferings.

Next, let us consider what may be useful to support and quieten our hearts under doubtful providences, when our dear concerns hang in a doubtful suspense before us, and we do not know which way the providence of God will cast and determine them.

Now the best hearts are apt to grow concerned and pensive, distracted with anxiety about the event and outcome. To relieve and settle us in this case, the following considerations are very useful.

Let us consider the vanity and uselessness of such anxiety. 'Which of you by taking thought can add one cubit unto his stature?' (Matt. 6. 27). We may break our peace and waste our spirits, but not alter the case. We cannot turn God out of His way. 'He is in one mind' (Job. 23. 13). We may, by struggling against God, increase, but not avoid or lighten our troubles.

How often do we afflict and torment ourselves by our own restless thoughts, when there is no real cause or ground for so doing? 'And hast feared continually every day because of the fury of the oppressor, as if he were ready to destroy; and where is the fury of the oppressor?' (Isa. 51. 13). O what abundance of disquiet and trouble might we prevent by waiting quietly till we see the issues of Providence, and not bringing as we do the evils of the morrow upon today?

How great a ground of quietness it is that the whole disposal and management of all our affairs and concerns is in the hand of our own God and Father. No creature can touch us without His commission or permission. 'Jesus answered, Thou couldest have no power at all against me, except it were given thee from above' (John 19. 11). Neither men nor devils can do anything without God's leave, and be sure He will sign no order to your prejudice.

How great satisfaction must it be to all that believe the divine authority of the Scripture that the faithfulness of God stands engaged for every line and syllable found therein! And how many blessed lines in the Bible may we mark, that respect even our outward concerns and the happy issue of them all!

Upon these two grounds, viz., that our outward concerns with their steady direction to a blessed end is found in the Word; and this Word being of divine authority, the faithfulness and honour of God stands good for every tittle that is found there; I say these are grounds of such stability that our minds may repose with the greatest security and confidence upon them, even in the cloudiest day of trouble. Not only your eternal salvation but your temporal interests are there secured. Be quiet therefore in the confidence of a blessed outcome.

How great and sure a means have the saints ever found it to their own peace, to commit all doubtful outcomes of Providence to the Lord, and devolve all their cares upon Him! 'Commit thy works unto the Lord, and thy thoughts shall be established' (Prov. 16. 3). By works he means any doubtful, intricate, perplexing business, about which our thoughts are racked and tortured. Roll all these upon the Lord by faith, leave them with Him, and the present immediate benefit you shall have by it, besides the comfort in the last issue, shall be tranquillity and peace in your thoughts. And who is there of any standing or experience in religion that has not found it so?

How may a Christian work his heart into resignation to the will of God when sad providences approach him and forebode great troubles and afflictions coming on towards him?

For the right stating and resolving of this important case it will be needful to show what is not included and intended in the question, what it does suppose and include in it, and what help and directions are necessary for the due performance of this great and difficult duty.

It must be premised that the question does not suppose the heart or will of a Christian to be at his own command and disposal in this matter. We cannot resign it, and subject it to the will of God whenever we desire so to do. The duty indeed is ours, but the power by which alone we perform it is God's; we act as we are acted upon by the Spirit. It is with our hearts as with meteors hanging in the air by the influence of the sun; while that continues they abide above, but when it fails they fall to the earth. We can do this and all things else, however difficult, through Christ that strengthens us (Phil. 4. 13). But without Him we can do nothing (John 15. 5). He does not say, Without me ye can do but little, or without me ye can do nothing but with great difficulty, or without me ye can do nothing perfectly, but 'without me ye can do nothing' at all. And every Christian has a witness in his own breast to attest this truth. For there are cases frequently occurring in the methods of Providence in which, notwithstanding all their prayers and desires, all their reasonings and strivings, they cannot quieten their hearts fully in the disposal and will of God; but on the contrary they find all their endeavours in this matter to be but as the rolling of a returning stone against the hill. Till God say to the heart, Be still, and to the will, Give up, nothing can be done.

Let us consider what this case does suppose and include in it, and we shall find that it supposes the people of God to have a foresight of troubles and distresses approaching and drawing near to them. I confess it is not always so, for many of our afflictions, as well as comforts, come upon us by way of surprise; but often we have forewarning of troubles, both public and personal, before we feel them. As the weather may be discerned by the face of the sky – when we see a morning sky red and lowring, this is a natural sign of a foul and rainy day (Matt. 16. 3) – so there are as certain signs of the times by which we may discern when trouble is near, even at the door. And these forewarnings are given by the Lord to awaken us to our duties, by which they may either be prevented (Zeph. 2. 1, 2), or sanctified and sweetened to us when they come. These signs and notices of approaching troubles are gathered partly from the observation and collation of parallel Scripture cases and examples, God generally holding one tenor and steady course in the administrations of His providences in all ages (1 Cor. 10. 6), and partly from the reflections Christians make upon the attitude and disposition of their own hearts, which greatly need awakening, humbling and purging providences. For let a Christian be but a few years or months without a rod, and how formal, earthly, dead and vain will his heart grow! And such a disposition presages affliction to them that are beloved of the Lord, as really as the giving or sweating of the stones does rain. Lastly, the ordering and disposing of the next causes into a posture and preparation for our trouble, plainly warns us that trouble is at the door. Thus when the symptoms of sickness begin to appear on our own bodies, the wife of our bosom, or our children, that are as our own souls, Providence herein awakens our expectations of death and doleful separations. So when enemies combine together and plot the ruin of our liberties, estates or lives, and God seems to loose the bridle of restraint upon their neck, we cannot but be alarmed with the near approach of troubles, especially when at the same time our conscience reflects upon the abuse and non-improvement of these our threatened comforts.

The case before us supposes that these premonitions and forerunners of affliction do usually very much disturb the order and break the peace of our souls; they put the mind under great discomposure, the thoughts under much distraction, and the affections into tumults and rebellion.

Ah, how unwilling we are to surrender to the Lord the loan which He lent us! to be disquieted by troubles when at ease in our enjoyments! How unwelcome are the messengers of affliction to the best men! We are ready to say to them as the widow to Elijah: 'What have I to do with thee, O thou man of God; art thou come unto me to call my sin to remembrance, and to slay my son?' (1 Kings 17. 18). And this arises partly from the remains of corruption in the best souls, for though every sanctified person is come by his own consent into the kingdom and under the government and sceptre of Christ, and every thought of his heart by right must be subjected to Him (2 Cor. 10. 5), yet in fact the conquest and power of grace is but incomplete and in part, and natural corruption, like Jeroboam with his vain men, rises up against it, and causes many mutinies in the soul, whilst grace, like young Abijah, is weak-handed and cannot resist them; and partly from the advantage Satan makes upon the season to irritate and assist our corruptions. He knows that what is already in motion is the more easily moved. In this confusion and hurry of thoughts he undiscernedly slips in his temptations, sometimes aggravating the evils which we fear with all the sinking and overwhelming circumstances imaginable, sometimes divining and forecasting such events and evils as, haply, never fall out, sometimes repining at the disposals of God as more severe to us than others, and sometimes reflecting with very unbelieving and unworthy thoughts upon the promises of God, and His faithfulness in them, by all which the affliction is made to sink deep into the soul before it actually comes. The thoughts are so disordered that duty cannot be duly performed. And the soul is really weakened and disabled to bear its trial when it comes indeed; just as if a man should be kept waking and restless all the night with the thoughts of his hard journey which he must travel to-morrow, and so when to-morrow is come he faints mid-way on his journey for want of rest.

It is here supposed to be the Christian's great duty, under the apprehensions of approaching troubles, to resign his will to God's and quietly commit the events and their outcome to Him, whatever they may prove. Thus did David in the like case and circumstances: 'And the king said unto Zadok, Carry back the ark of God into the city; if I shall find favour in the eyes of the Lord, he will bring me back again, and show me both it and his habitation: But if he thus say, I have no delight in thee: behold here am I, let him do to me as seemeth good unto him' (2 Sam. 15. 25, 26). O lovely and truly Christian attitude! As much as to say, Go Zadok, return with the ark to its place; though I have not the symbol, yet I hope I shall have the real presence of God with me in this sad journey. How He will dispose the events of this sad and doubtful providence I know not. Either I shall return again to Jerusalem, or I shall not. If I do, then I shall see it again, and enjoy the Lord in His ordinances there. If I do not, then I shall go to that place where there is no need or use of those things. And either way it will be well for me. I am content to refer all to the divine pleasure, and commit the issue, be it whatever it will, to the Lord.

And till our hearts come to the like resolve, we can have no peace within. 'Commit thy works unto the Lord, and thy thoughts shall be established' (Prov. 16. 3). By works he means not only every enterprise and business we undertake, but every puzzling, intricate and doubtful event we fear. These being once committed by an act of faith, and our wills resigned to His, besides the comfort we shall have in the issue, we shall have the present advantage of a well-composed and peaceful spirit.

But this resignation is the difficulty. There is no doubt of peace, could we once bring our hearts to that. And therefore I shall here give such helps and directions as may, through God's blessing and in the faithful use of them, assist and facilitate this great and difficult work.

Labour to work into your hearts a deep and fixed sense of the infinite wisdom of God and your own folly and ignorance. This will make resignation easy to you. Whatsoever the Lord does is by counsel (Eph. 1. 11), His understanding is infinite (Ps. 147. 5), His thoughts are very deep (Ps. 92. 5), but as for man, yea, the wisest among men, how little does his understanding penetrate the works and designs of Providence! And how often we are forced to retract our rash opinions and confess our mistakes, and to acknowledge that if Providence had not seen with better eyes than ours, and looked farther than we did, we had precipitated ourselves into a thousand mischiefs, which by its wisdom and care we have escaped. It is well for us that the 'seven eyes of Providence' are ever awake and looking out for our good. Now if one creature can and ought to be guided and governed by another that is more wise and skilful than himself, as the client by his learned counsel, the patient by his skilful physician, much more should every one give up his weak reason and shallow understanding to the infinite and omniscient God.

It is nothing but our pride and arrogance over-valuing our own understandings that makes resignation so hard. Carnal

reason seems to itself a wise disputant about the concerns of
the flesh, but how often has Providence baffled it! The more
humility, the more resignation.

How few of our mercies and comforts have been foreseen
by us! Our own projects have come to nothing, and that which
we never thought of or contrived has taken place; not our
choice of the ground, or skill in weighing and delivering the
bowl, but some unforeseen providence, like a rub in the green,
was that which made the cast.

Deeply consider the sinfulness and vanity of torturing your
own thoughts about the issues of doubtful providences.

There is much sin in so doing, for all our anxious and
agitated emotions, what are they other than the immediate
outcome and fruits of pride and unbelief? There is not a
greater display of pride in the world than in the contests of
our wills with the will of God. It is a presumptuous invading
of God's prerogative to dictate to His providence and prescribe
to His wisdom.

There is a great deal of vanity in it. All the thoughtfulness in
the world will not make one hair white or black. All our dis-
contents will not prevail with God to call back, or as the word
may be rendered, make void His Word (Isa. 31. 2). He is in one
mind (Job 23. 13), the thoughts of His mind are from everlasting (Ps. 33. 11).

Set before you those choice Scripture patterns of submission
to the Lord's will in as deep, yea, much deeper points of self-
denial than this before you, and shame yourselves out of this
quarrelling attitude with Providence.

You know what a close trial that providence was to Abraham, that called him from his native country and father's
house to go he knew not where; and yet it is said that he came
to God's foot, as readily obeying his call as a servant when his
master knocks for him with his foot (Isa. 41. 2).

Paul's voyage to Jerusalem had a dismal aspect upon himself. He could expect nothing but bonds and prisons, as he tells
us (Acts 20. 23), and a great trial it was to the saints, who
could not tell how to give up such a minister; yet he resigns

up his will to God's (20. 22), and so do they: 'The will of the Lord be done' (21. 14).

But far beyond these, and all other patterns, what an example has our dear Lord Jesus set before us in the deepest point of self-denial that ever was in the world! When the Father gave the cup of sufferings into His hands in the garden, a cup of wrath, the wrath of the great and terrible God, and that without mixture, the very taste of which put nature into an agony and astonishment, a sore amazement, a bloody sweat, and forced from him that vehement and sad cry: 'Abba, Father, all things are possible unto thee; take away this cup from me'; yet still with submission, 'nevertheless not what I will, but what thou wilt' (Mark 14. 36). O blessed pattern of obedience and resignation to the pleasure of God! What is your case in comparison to this?

Study the singular benefits and advantages of a will resigned up and melted into the will of God.

Such a spirit has a continual Sabbath within itself. The thoughts are established (Prov. 16. 3), and truly, till a man come to this, he does but too much resemble the devil, who is a restless spirit seeking rest but finding none. It was an excellent expression of Luther to one that was much perplexed in his spirit about the doubtful events of some affairs of his that were then depending: 'The Lord shall do all for thee, and thou shalt do nothing but be the Sabbath of Christ.' It is by this means that the Lord 'giveth his beloved sleep' (Ps. 127. 2); he does not mean the sleep of the body, but of the spirit. As one has said on this verse: 'Though believers live in the midst of many troubles here, yet with quiet and composed minds they keep themselves in the silence of faith, as though they were asleep.'

Besides, it fits a man's spirit for communion with God in all his afflictions, and this alleviates and sweetens them beyond anything in the world.

And surely a man is never nearer the mercy he desires, or the deliverance he expects, as one truly observes, than when his soul is brought into a submissive attitude. David was never nearer the kingdom than when he became as a weaned child.

Think how repugnant an unsubmissive attitude is both to your prayers and professions.

You pray that the will of God may be done on earth as it is in heaven, and yet when it seems contrary to your will or interest, you struggle or fret against it. You profess to have committed your souls to His keeping, and to leave your eternal concerns in His hands, and yet cannot commit things infinitely less valuable unto Him. How contradictory are these things!

You profess as Christians to be led by the Spirit, but this practice shows you follow the perverse counsels of your own spirits. O then, regret no more, dispute no more, but lie down meekly at your Father's feet, and say in all cases and at all times, 'The will of the Lord be done.'

And thus I have, through the aid of Providence, performed what I designed to speak from this Scripture. I acknowledge that my performances have been accompanied with much weakness, yet I have endeavoured to speak of Providence the things that are right. Blessed be the Lord who has thus far assisted and protected me in this work.

How Providence will dispose of my life, liberty and labours for time to come, I know not; but I cheerfully commit all to Him who has hitherto performed all things for me (Ps. 57. 2).

13

THE ADVANTAGES OF RECORDING OUR
EXPERIENCES OF PROVIDENCE

In consideration of the great and manifold advantages result-
ing from a humble and careful observation of Providence, I
cannot but judge it the concern of Christians that have time
and ability for such a work, to keep written memorials or
journals of Providence by them; for their own and others' use
and benefit. For want of collecting and communicating such
observations, not only ourselves, but the Church of God is
greatly impoverished.

Some say the art of medicine was acquired and perfected
thus. When anyone had met with some rare medicinal herb,
and accidentally discovered the virtues of it, he would post it
up in some public place; and so the physician attained his skill
by a collection of those posted experiments and recipes.

I am not for posting up all that a Christian knows or meets
with in his experience, for, as I have said before, religion does
not lay all open; yet there is a prudent, humble and seasonable
communication of our experiences and observations of Providence which is exceeding beneficial both to ourselves and our
brethren.

If Christians in reading the Scriptures would judiciously
collect and record the providences they shall meet with there,
and (if destitute of other helps) but add those that have fallen
out in their own time and experience, O what a precious
treasure would these make! What an antidote would it be to
their souls against the spreading atheism of these days, and

satisfy them beyond what many other arguments can do, that 'The Lord he is the God; the Lord he is the God' (1 Kings 18. 39).

Whilst this work was under my hand, I was both delighted and assisted by a pious and useful essay of an unknown author, who has to very good purpose used many Scriptural passages of Providence which seem to lie out of the road of common observation. Some passages I have noted out of it which have been sweet to me. O that Christians would everywhere set themselves to such work! Providence carries our lives, liberties and concerns in its hand every moment. Your bread is in its cupboard, your money in its purse, your safety in its enfolding arms; and surely it is the least part of what you owe to record the favours you receive at its hands.

Do not trust your slippery memories with such a multitude of remarkable passages of Providence as you have, and shall meet with in your way to heaven. It is true, things that greatly affect us are not easily forgotten by us; and yet, how ordinary is it for new impressions to raze out former ones? It was a saying of that worthy man, Dr Harris: 'My memory never failed me in all my life; for indeed, I durst never trust it.' Written memorials secure us against that hazard, and besides, make them useful to others when we are gone, so that you do not carry away all your treasure to heaven with you, but leave these choice legacies to your surviving friends. Certainly it were not so great a loss to lose your silver, your goods and chattels, as it is to lose your experiences which God has this way given you in this world.

Take heed of clasping up those rich treasures in a book, and thinking it enough to have noted them there; but have frequent recourse to them, as oft as new needs, fears or difficulties arise and assault you. Now it is seasonable to consider and reflect, Was I never so distressed before? Is this the first plunge that ever befell me? Let me consider the days of old, the years of ancient times, as Asaph did (Ps. 77. 5).

Beware of slighting former straits and dangers in comparison with present ones. That which is next to us always appears greatest to us, and as time removes us farther and farther from our former mercies or dangers, so they grow less in our eyes, just as the land does from those who sail. Know that your dangers have been as great, and your fears no less formerly than now. Make it as much your business to preserve the sense and value as the memory of former providences, and the fruit will be sweet to you.

THE REFORMATION IN ENGLAND

J. H. Merle d'Aubigné

'It may be that in this land of ours in years to
come gospel ministers will become scarce
enough. If the popery which now abounds in
the Church of England is to go on increasing
the day may come when the voice of Christian ministry will be silenced by law, and
persecution allowed to rage; for, be not deceived, Rome has not changed her views; and
let her once get power again, all the penal
laws will be re-enacted, and you Protestants
who are today flinging away your liberties as
dirt cheap will rue the day in which you
allowed the old chains to be fitted upon your
wrists. Popery fettered and slew our sires,
and yet we are making it the national religion. . . .' These prophetic words, uttered by
C. H. Spurgeon in 1876, were never nearer
their fulfilment than today. The times cry
loudly for a thorough-going acquaintance
with the Reformation.

Volume 1 – From the introduction of Christianity to Britain to 1530. 498 pages. Illustrated.

Volume 2 – From 1530 to 1547. 524 pages.
Illustrated.

Paperback 7/6. Bound edition 21/–.